"As a conventionally traine[d ...] there is much more to help [... chal]lenges than blood test, x-rays, and drugs. I have worked with Patti for a decade and have witnessed the impact of energetic and emotional healing on our patients and especially patients in whom conventional therapies had limited effectiveness. This book is a great introduction, even for skeptics to get a sampling of the power of these therapies."

—Frenesa Hall, M.D.

"What an incredible book by America's foremost medical intuitive and vibrational healer, Patti Conklin. She has written a manual on how life *really* works, weaving her unique life experiences into short stories to enhance understanding."

—Dick Sutphen, author of *You Were Born Again to Be Together*

"I had the amazing privilege to learn about and experience Patti's extraordinary gifts and energy medicine in 2006. I experienced Patti's revolutionary one-of-a-kind healing modality Cellular Cleansing and my health and consciousness around becoming my own best healer was transformed in miraculous ways above and beyond my wildest dreams. I'm a filmmaker and I am now promoting around the world a documentary film I co-produced entitled *Bipolarized*. It is a film that shares a holistic perspective of how we can all heal the root causes of our mental health symptoms. Meeting Patti is a huge reason why this film became a reality for me to create. In my experience Patti is not only a beautiful soul but also one of the most powerful healers of our time. It is an honor to have crossed paths with Patti on my journey of healing and self-discovery."

—Ross McKenzie, filmmaker, co-producer of *Bipolarized*

GOD WITHIN

THE DAY GOD'S TRAIN STOPPED

PATTI CONKLIN

RAINBOW RIDGE
BOOKS

Cover and interior design by Frame25 Productions

Published by:
Rainbow Ridge Books, LLC
140 Rainbow Ridge Road
Faber, Virginia 22938
434-361-1723

If you are unable to order this book from your local
bookseller, you may order directly from the distributor.

Square One Publishers, Inc.
115 Herricks Road
Garden City Park, NY 11040
Phone: (516) 535-2010
Fax: (516) 535-2014
Toll-free: 877-900-BOOK

Visit the author at:
www.patticonklin.com

Library of Congress Cataloging-in-Publication Data applied for.

ISBN 978-1-937907-23-5

10 9 8 7 6 5 4 3 2 1

Printed on acid-free recycled paper in the United States of America

CONTENTS

ACKNOWLEDGEMENTS

DANIEL CONKLIN AND MATTHEW CONKLIN, words cannot express my love and respect for you both. As my sons, you are my greatest accomplishments. I take great pride in the boys that you were and the men that you've become. You show a depth of flexibility, understanding, and acceptance of life that is a constant inspiration for me. My work took me to the road many days of your childhood, and you took my physical absence in stride. You missed me, but you never judged or held disappointment in me. You are the reason that this book exists; that my work exists.

Daniel, you provided sage guidance and have always boldly and assuredly expressed to me "your view" with a level of respect and love that even I find difficult to match. Matthew, you've provided day-to-day assistance in my work and without your hands-on help, your understanding of vibration, your compassion, and your keen ability to take over both administrative responsibilities and emotional support for those in need, my work would have stalled years ago. I am honored beyond measure to be your mom.

Daniel, Matthew, Russell, and Tony: you each have given time, love, support, and expertise during your high school years, years when you would rather that I had dropped you at the mall to hang with friends, you instead assisted me in making products, answering phones, and helping out as much as you could. Your selflessness during that time is deeply appreciated and I honor each of you with love.

Vanessa, your female presence and nurturing as a big sister helped me to shape the men in our family into the wonderful, caring individuals they are today. Plus your culinary skills are the best this family's ever seen! Michael, your big brother presence and priceless guidance to all of the boys with continued unwavering support well into their adult lives assisted them in painting their own canvas. Because of you both, Vanessa and Michael, all four boys were given encouragement that allowed them the esteem to establish their own ideas, dreams, goals, and ambitions. You both provided to them the gift of an open forum to flourish and transform into their own uniqueness; a gift that only older siblings can give. My love, thanks, and respect to you both overflow.

Howard, Kylen, and Emmett, my family continues to grow with you, my grandsons. One day, your dear Oma will share dozens of stories of your beautiful and colorful family. Some stories may make you laugh. Some will make you cry. Some will make your parents groan. These stories, though, are stories of your heritage; of your moms and dads, your cousins and friends, and your Oma. Take these stories and pull them in tight and dear, for it is in these stories that we may pass wisdom from our generation to yours.

As a woman, I have had wonderful adventures, relationships, and experiences which have only enhanced my gift and my ability to be who I am today. Tony Whitehead, thank you for your quips of wisdom, for believing in me and caring enough to provide gentle summaries and observations, which forced me to stop my train of thought and rethink how I view life. You taught me that it was okay to occasionally stop that strong desire to climb the mountain and learn to play and just be a woman. You will always be a giant in my little corner of the world. Thank you for our friendship and your continued input in my life. It is cherished.

Melanie Boock, Lane Diamond, Daniel Conklin, and all others who assisted me with this endeavor, thank you for working your way through this manuscript. As Dan so aptly asked with much humor, "Mom, do you even know what a paragraph is?"

Lastly, I'd like to thank each and every one of my friends, clients, physicians, scientists, and colleagues. All of you have assisted in my growth, my understanding of vibrational medicine and medical intuition. My ability to grow and expand my gift, my womanhood, my humanity has occurred because of you.

I give thanks to you, God, for this beautiful life that YOU have chosen to bless me with. I know I am not perfect, Father, far from it, but I endeavor to continue my growth and being of service to all.

INTRODUCING THE INTRODUCTION

by D. T. Conklin

I was recently asked what I love about my mother, Patti Conklin, and I answered with this: One of the things I was taught as a child, and something I still learn with every day that passes, is unconditional love. However, if I'm supposed to pick out things I love about her, as opposed to things I don't love, doesn't that then make it conditional? I think it does, and the reason I think that is because of my mother. She taught me what unconditional love means, even when it's nearly impossible to describe.

So I could go on here and list things about her that I love, such as how she's caring, and giving, and loving, and always puts other people first. I could talk about how I can call her at 3 a.m. and still know she'll answer, no matter what's going on. Or how she's never judged me, always stood by me, and never for an instant stopped loving me. Sure, I love these things about her. But what I love more is what she's done for my life, simply by being who she is—and that's not something that can be stuffed into a single word, or three words, or even a thousand. That's a state of being, and as such it's nearly indescribable.

The things I love about her exist through a lifetime, not defined by words.

What is a life? It's a series of stories, a series of experiences, all crammed together to form something greater than those pieces. In a way, it's a lesson. It's something and nothing, always screaming, always quiet, and it's something we can't label. This book is hers.

INTRODUCTION

by Patti Conklin

I'm not sure how to start this, except to go to the beginning. That's the way of stories, isn't it?

My life changed forever at the age of seven. I was upstairs, alone in my bedroom and playing with a piece of rope, cat's cradle, which was a favorite alone time game, when a white mist seeped from the walls. Like a deep fog it rolled from the paint, the wood beneath, the base of the windowsill. It slid forward, at first silent and white, but within seconds sound and color drifted from it.

I fell to my knees, not because I was scared, but because it was the right thing to do. I'd not felt that type of serenity before, but I've felt exactly the same way each and every time I've had what I classify as a visitation since then. A male voice, who I've since always called Father, told me three things;

1. My greatest growth years would be between thirty-eight and forty-two.

2. My greatest work would be between forty-two and sixty-two.

3. My purpose would be to teach people how to become insubstantial without transitioning.

Yeah, I had no idea what that meant.

And yet life went on.

Skip ahead.

At the age of twelve, I realized my parents couldn't understand me. So I stayed away from home more and more, sitting on the fabulous street corners of Ithaca, NY, seeing people's words form in their brains, and then watching them zigzag into their bodies. Of course, I didn't know that normal people didn't see these things.

I was . . . different.

Skip further ahead.

I married at nineteen, and had my sons Daniel and Matthew at twenty-four and twenty-five. A few years after they were born, my husband and I divorced. He was a good man, and still is, but it was clear we were never a match. In my view of the world, we had come together for our sons. I believe that the soul chooses the parents for the lessons of the current incarnation, and that people come together for that very purpose.

I have a hundred different stories I could tell about myself, many of which I will relate in the following pages of this book. You see, stories have a greater importance than we realize. They teach us substantial lessons, but they also teach the insubstantial. They allow us to look at another's experience and apply it to our own lives. More than that, they allow us to delve deeper into ourselves. They allow us to ask questions. They allow us to grow. And I believe my greatest life lessons stemmed from my sons, Daniel and Matthew.

This introduction, which gives a glimpse of my life, is best focused on them.

Daniel, the eldest, comes first. He watched everything as a baby—the way steam rose from a pot of boiling water, the bees zipping around in a garden of roses and lilacs, down to the way pieces of a puzzle fit together to form a whole. He spoke in full sentences at the age of fourteen months, and was incredibly articulate for his age.

At the time, I hadn't yet thought about past lives or Karma, what was right or what was wrong . . . it didn't make sense that people reincarnated.

One day, he was wiping off the breakfast bar with a sponge, one of his favorite things to do. On and on he wiped, and as he continued, I finally said, "Dan, I think you've done a great job. It looks like it's all done."

To which he replied, "My other Mommy always let me wipe it as much as I wanted."

His other . . . ? "Who is your other Mommy?"

He laid the sponge down and looked me straight in the eye, and it was the first time a chill ever coursed down my back. "Obviously I need to explain something to you. It took God a little bit of time to get you and Daddy ready for me, so he gave me another Mommy and Daddy to live with."

I must admit, I gasped a bit, because it had taken us five years to conceive him.

"I still remember her hugs," he said, wrapping his arms around himself. "I really don't remember my other Daddy, but I remember her hugs. Her hugs . . . I was nine when the car hit me, but it didn't hurt. You and Daddy were ready."

I don't know what else I can say about that; it speaks for itself.

Today he's the sage, the one with an insight that even I haven't developed, and I constantly learn from him. He has a nasty habit of looking at me, immediately recognizing a problem, and giving me the solution. I don't always like it. Indeed, I rarely like it. But because I hold such deep respect for him, I always contemplate what he says, not that I always follow what he suggests. Sometimes it takes me weeks or months to realize he's right, but, more often than not, he is.

He was incredibly protective of his brother, Matthew, who came sixteen months later. He would proudly, and very seriously, announce to anyone who came to the door that "Meem" was sleeping, and they'd better not wake him up.

Matthew was six weeks premature, so he didn't develop as quickly as his brother. He was wired differently. He hadn't received my sight; rather, he shared my energy capabilities. Even from a very young age, he could touch where I was hurting, and the pain would stop.

When he was a young man, about twelve or so, I was working with a board member who was in a lot of elbow pain from wheeling around in her wheelchair. He came into the room and placed his hands on my shoulder, and a massive heat struck my shoulder. I looked at him and suggested that he create intent to allow that energy to go down my arm into my hands in order to assist me.

He gave me an angry look and said, "I'm new at this, you know!"

All I could do was laugh.

Skip ahead again.

My life, my work, has its downsides. I was gone a lot, and I'm sure my sons dealt with it in ways I'm unaware of. I will never forget when Matt was in high school; I believe he was a junior. He'd left for school, and I received a call from a woman who was dying—I had promised her that I would honor a request to be there as she passed, and I booked a flight to San Francisco.

So I did what any mother would do: I left a note on the fridge.

That evening, I was boarding the redeye back to Atlanta, and called home to check on things. Matthew answered, and I asked him how his day was. He said, "Well, Mom, glad you asked. I had the worst day of my life, and the only thing that kept me together was knowing I could come home, and that you'd put your arms around me, and everything would be okay . . . And you're not here."

I cried a lot that night.

He was right. I wasn't there. And, while he wasn't angry, his point was well taken.

Daniel is co-founder of Evolved Publishing, and has written his own book, *Eulogy*, an epic fantasy. It's humorous to me, because while he doesn't agree, so much of his writing is derived from questions he asked as a child. Could God actually have a father? What if we're just pawns that He moves around?

Matthew is the closest to me in the gift of energy, and he's been the executive director of Healing Within for many years. He's my go-to guy when I need help with workshops, live video, or cellular cleansings. His energy, his ability to help someone through an emotional process, takes my breath away. While he doesn't feel that this will be his life work, he is definitely my lifeline when I need it.

I've called myself many things: mother, daughter, sister, lover, student, employee, boss, hypnotherapist, light worker, medical intuitive, vibrational mediator. In all of this, what I've come to realize at fifty-five years old, is that the purpose, this quest I feel I am on, driven by what Father first told me, "Help people become insubstantial without transitioning," is really, "Help people become unconditional without having to die to do it."

Obviously, I am not perfect. I screw up, and I've endured hard lessons in order to grow—I've lost friendships because of my behavior; I've lost lovers because I wasn't able to put my work aside. Yet I do understand the need to continually ask myself, "Am I in my integrity? Am I being honest with myself? Am I out of ego and judgment?"

Of course, I could be totally wrong . . . .

Father could be sitting up there, watching me, shaking his head and saying, "What the heck is she *doing* down there? I simply asked her to wash the windows!"

And so my story begins.

WORD POWER

In the beginning was the Word. The Word
was with God, and the Word was God.
—John 1:1

I BELIEVE THAT WHEN the universe began, words did not
exist. A cacophony of tones, which we now identify as frequency, echoed throughout the universe, and they were both
chaotic and highly ordered. Long, long ago, at the time of
the very first spark, the very first light, all souls broke away
from what we consider God, existing in spirit form, outside
of judgment and ego. They didn't speak. They didn't hear.
They simply were.

So how did we morph into this dense flesh?

That's simple, and yet very complicated. As our souls
evolved, we began to use words to express ourselves, and we
started to respond emotionally to our circumstances. A word
is such a small, insignificant thing, and yet it's so much more.
It represents emotion, and emotion is the cornerstone of our
physical existence.

In a nutshell, we became conditional.

We're happy when someone tells us we're accomplished.

We're sad when someone tells us we've failed.

So what's *unconditional*?

No matter what happens, no matter what you might
say or do to me, I'll love you. Let the oceans rise, let the
lightning fall and strike and blast, and still I'll hold you
dear. Forever. No matter what.

Caring for the weak, or sick, regardless if they can do
something in return. Doing it regardless of whether they
deserve it or not.

But why are some things conditional? I believe they have
a judgment, or an ego, attached to them. Words allow emotions—conditional, unconditional, loving, and fearing—to
manifest. Think of it this way: the words we use to express
judgment affect the ultra-fast vibration of the spirit form. But
those vibrations slow and solidify when we dwell within judgment and ego, and words stand at the heart. This means that,
long ago, spirits evolved into solid physical forms, thus mark-
ing the beginning of life as we know it.

And the Word was made flesh.
—John 1:14

So now we understand how words and emotions work
together to evolve us into physical beings, but let's explore the
idea more. Imagine a whisper of light and tone, floating with
no form, an essence of purity. It evolves the ability to think, to
reason, to love and fear, and those things are orchestrated by

words. Conditional words transform our souls into a physical form. They're dense, they're heavy, and at that very instant, the spirit becomes a conditional being. It has shed its unconditional self like water from a leaf, and it has taken conditional form. Words have a simple yet profound effect on everyone's life, and I believe there are no exceptions.

2

WE ARE WHAT WE SAY

.

IN CHAPTER 1, WE learned how words make us into conditional beings. They're part of us, down to our very core, and now we'll learn how they affect our lives and our health.

I've spent countless hours observing human behavior, and this is where it's important to define my gift. More than simply watching people sip their coffee, or talk about the latest football game, I'm able to literally watch words form in people's brains. These words look like beautiful hanging plants, located in the Heart Center Chakra, or, in science, known as the Thymus Gland. Tiny tendrils flow from them, and they reach into every single cell of the immune system.

However, what people feel and what they think are often two different things. Take this as an example, and I know we've all done it:

> My emotional thought says, "Oh no, here comes Tom."
> But my voice says, "Tom! It's so great to see you!"

Yikes! Two sets of emotions, two sets of phrases, and neither of them like the other. Yet, you know what? You guessed it. They both reach into the body, and they both have equal strength. Like waves rippling, they surge through the immune system, then store in individual cells.

So what's truly the most important piece to take away from that? To me, it's the phrase immune system, otherwise known as the subtle energy field (our originating energy). Whether spoken or thought, all types of words are stored in the immune system, and, as we previously learned, they are heavy things. They're dense, an integral part of us down to our very core.

Now that we understand our immune system's relation to words, we're able to introduce the concept of disease. How is it created? Why do we get sick? And just as important, how is it healed?

In our above example, I didn't want to see Tom, and yet I told him how good it was to see him. My body stored two sets of conflicting words and emotions at the same time. This is the beginning of disease. When a word is attached to a conditional emotion, it is still stored in the body, and the word creates a vibrational blockage unique to every person.

Visualize with me for a moment: imagine energy flowing in your body like the water in a creek. It runs at a certain rate in cubic feet per minute. If someone jams a log in the creek, the water dams up. The log isn't moving at the same rate as the creek, and so the water must flow around it. You might never notice the slight variation from a single log. However, if more logs are piled on, and a heavy rain pummels the area, then the increased rate of water could cause a flood. Before you know it, a whole field is underwater.

People may not notice an emotional blockage until the rain pours down, and a flood creates disease or illness. Maybe they lose their job, or split from their spouse, or maybe it's simply an accumulation of little things, and they allow fear and ego to take precedence. They then wonder how everything became stopped up.

The only way to rid ourselves of blockages is to remove them with a vibration identical to that of the words' vibration at the time of storage. Visualize this example: we store blockages in a lockbox, and the key is a vibration. Thus, we must find the same vibration to unlock that box, even if we do so years later.

It's important to note that neutral words simply merge with the vibration of our bodies. They don't cause blockages, nor do they remove them, as even the most neutral of words can only preserve the status quo. In the end, removing conditional emotions and words inside of a cell requires an active vibration, something that will literally shake the cell and release the blockages.

Our ability to set and maintain healthy perceptions is the key to our physical and emotional wellness, for how we speak and feel is literally absorbed into our cells.

To reiterate: perception of your life, and the world around you, changes your mind and body—the two are not separate. Every word, no matter the source, has been absorbed into your cellular memory, with the potential to increase your vulnerability to disease.

What you say and think, even if it is about someone else, is stored in your body as if you were speaking about yourself. Your cells have no discernment capabilities; they can't tell the difference between the *me* and the *them*. Thus, if you think or say:

> "Wow, Sally looks terrible today."
> "Mark is so mean. I wish he were nicer."

. . . your body stores it.

These are simplified examples, of course, but our cells believe we look terrible, and wish we looked better. They believe we're mean, and wish we were nicer. Our bodies begin to jam those logs in the creek, waiting for the flood.

I didn't know it early in life, but the Word, and the emotions attached to those words, would become the cornerstone of my life's work.

We are, quite literally, what we say.

3

A STORY TITLED "MY LIFE"

As a child, I suffered many typical maladies: earaches, fevers, colds, etc. Despite that, I maintained a healthy, active lifestyle until my late twenties, when I developed both forms of the autoimmune deficiency disease Lupus, which is an incurable, untreatable illness.

It was an incredibly challenging time in my life.

My sons were little, and I was a single mom attempting to create a good life for my children, working diligently in non-profit organizations. Yet I was so sick I could barely get out of bed. Painful flare-ups attacked my joints, and some days simply walking to the mailbox would stiffen them so badly that I couldn't move the next day.

I remember looking at myself in the mirror, watching my face as welts rose and yellow ooze seeped from them. My nervous system was so inflamed that putting on clothes was excruciating, and I would simply stand in the middle of the room, crying, naked, not able to sit down for hours at a time.

I truly wanted to die as exhaustion overtook me.

My doctors advised me that, given the severity of both forms of Lupus, I would only live another six to eight years. As time went on, I managed to cope, but I constantly questioned myself: why did this happen to me? How would I provide for my children? And, at the edge of it all, a little voice asked, "Are my doctors right?"

Then it struck me.

I was successful, a high school graduate working with people who all had Ph.D.s. Yet they were better than me, or so I thought. They were more deserving than me, or so I thought. I didn't deserve to be where I was, or so I thought . . . .

I had a self-worth issue. I didn't feel that I deserved my success, or indeed, even qualified to do the work I was involved with.

After three years of suffering, yet functioning with my Lupus, I had an experience that changed my perception.

≈

I had a dream one night.

The darkness outside was frigid, almost repressing, and the air within my bedroom was little better. I was brittle, fragile, something that would shatter if touched. Sleep eluded me, and I tossed and turned on the bed, twisting in and out of consciousness, cringing at every motion.

A light appeared—within myself—enveloping the whole room. I can't remember its exact origin inside, but it felt safe, similar to my first visitation at the age of seven, and so I dove within.

Father spoke to me, but not with words. Instead He spoke in color, in vibration, and in a way I was actually able to hear it—first blue, then white, and even a hint of blackness. They coursed through my body, each flashing and vanishing, only to be replaced by another. And yet, with each flash my body vibrated. More than that, my cells vibrated as those colors shook my worthiness issues away.

When I awoke that morning, part of me felt clearer. It was as if . . . I'm not sure how to describe it—like a pot that's been cleaned, or a car that's been scrubbed, sanded, and painted. I sat down to meditate, closed my eyes, and took a deep, deep breath. Instinct drove me at that point, as part of me recognized what Father had done, and what he wanted me to do.

I asked myself, "What color do I need to remove my Lupus?"

The colors flashed before me, and I sent each of them within myself, searching, waiting as they shook the sickness from my body. Yet despite the exercise, the rest of my day passed just as the days before it had passed—my muscles started to ache, my mind grew weak and foggy, and I experienced difficulty seeing.

Why had Father shown me this exercise if it wasn't going to work?

Then I realized my mistake: the "*issue in my tissue*" was not Lupus, it was my lack of self-worth. I didn't need to address my pain, or my disease, or any of those other things. I needed to increase my self-worth!

And so, yet again, I sat quietly, with my eyes closed, taking in deep breaths, relaxing my body completely, and asked myself, "What color do I need to increase myself self-worth?"

I expected vibrant colors to flash—beautiful whites, or sparkling green, or a subtle lilac. However, instead of seeing color, I heard a voice say, "Black."

What? Black?

All sorts of misconceptions flooded in—black was evil, dark. Yet misconceptions are simply that, and I quickly realized that I needed frequency, not someone else's description of color.

And so I simply trusted.

I breathed in through my nose and imagined blackness seeping through the bottom of my feet, up my body and out my mouth, just as Father had shown me. For me, personally, I didn't see it; I simply perceived it moving through my body. Ten minutes later, when I got up out of my meditation pose and began to walk around, I felt lighter, with more mental clarity.

The next day I asked again, "What color do I need to increase my self-worth?" And this time, I also asked, "What color do I need to remove my Lupus?"

It wasn't just about the emotional, at that point, and part of me recognized that. Once my words and lack of self-worth had manifested into disease, they also needed to be addressed. And so I addressed them.

I felt better with each day that passed, and I haven't experienced another active period since. My body felt good and comfortable, and all of my blood work was normal one year later, and continues to be so to this day.

Color works because it is an active vibration. As I said earlier, there are two active vibrations in the universe: color and tone. All other vibrations—crystals, essential oils, reiki, etc.—while important, are passive, which means that they don't have the frequency necessary to shake loose cellular memory.

I've used my form of ColorWorks and ToneWorks on over 100,000 people from around the world. It's amazing to work with someone and, within ten minutes, have them feel totally different—to be clarified, to be out of pain.

What a simple process for such dramatic results!

4

IT'S ABOUT HIS LIVER

PEOPLE ALWAYS ASK HOW my work applies to them. How is it made real? What does it really mean? Well, for all three of those questions, I can only show examples. What each person takes from these is her own, and different for us all.

The following story is from one of my first sessions, with a young man we'll call William.

~

William felt pressure on his liver. He'd visited his physician, and they did a series of blood work, CAT scans, and ultrasounds, attempting to find the core issue. However, the results came back inconclusive, and after much discomfort and no solutions, William turned to alternative medicine.

We'd spent approximately twenty minutes on the phone, at which time he asked, "How can you see me?" His voice was scratchy, slightly disbelieving, as if this were the last thing he wanted to be doing.

I understood his hesitation, and answered with a soft, soothing tone. "There's no such thing as time and space in terms of vibration. If you were sitting in India, to me it would be the same as if you were sitting here . . . ."

He grunted a little, neither an acceptance nor rebuttal, and then told me about his life currently—personally, professionally, and physically. It was exactly what one would expect: a certain amount of success here, a stumbling block there, and nothing to indicate any type of serious illness.

His body told me a different story, and I asked him to talk about life growing up. Five years old—nothing. Eight years old—nothing. Ten, twelve, and fourteen—nothing. As he reached the age of sixteen, life was wonderful: he was captain of the football team; he owned his own car; he appreciated a great relationship with his parents; and he had a wonderful girlfriend. He continued on to seventeen, but the word stop was written across his liver.

"Go back," I said. "Tell me again about sixteen."

I could almost see him roll his eyes, but he again spoke of the relationship with his parents, his experiences on the football team, his shiny new car, and his girlfriend. His girlfriend. His girlfriend.

"Ahh," I said. "Is that all that happened to you at sixteen?"

His voice grew cold, hard. "What?"

"Exactly what happened to you six months ago, when the pressure began? Was there anything that stood out that you were frustrated and angry about?"

He was still angry, his words short and curt, but he played along. I've always imagined that he cracked a pencil in half as he said, "Well, I was at a family picnic, having some quiet time with my sister, and she confessed that she'd had an abortion earlier in the year. She hadn't told me about it. Me, her brother! She hadn't taken me into her confidences, hadn't let me help her through—"

"Do you feel . . . ?" I waited for him to calm down before I continued. "Could there be a correlation between your sister's abortion and the abortion your girlfriend had when you were sixteen?"

Silence filled the phone.

"How could you have possibly known that? No one knows about that."

"Your liver knows it. It's where you stored the memory of your girlfriend having an abortion, without speaking to you, without asking how you felt about it, and you found out after the fact. Remember how angry you were? You stored it within your liver. In addition, when you found out about your sister having an abortion, and you not being informed, the anger that was already stored in your liver created more density. You can equate it to the straw that broke the camel's back."

He sputtered, obviously unsure if he should believe me. Worse than that, he probably didn't know what to do if I was right. His fear was so obvious, it bled through the phone. What if he, or I, couldn't fix this? What if it was too late? Would he die, here, this week or next, or the month after it?

I asked him to close his eyes. "What color does your body need to remove the anger from your liver?"

Again he was silent for a moment. "It's . . . it's similar to molasses, kind of a brownish color, but thick and heavy."

"Breathe in through your nose. Imagine pulling the color through the bottom of your feet, into your body, up your calves and into your thighs, your hips, your abdomen and midsection, including your liver. Push the color out of your mouth."

The colors changed as he did this—first the brown, then an oozing green, then a silent blue, and finally white with tinges of gray at the edges. It continued for a minute, then two, and then four.

I said, "Imagine white light seeping into all the pores of your body, just healing and cleansing, healing and cleansing. Now what color do you need to fully balance? It can be a rainbow, two or three colors, or simply one color."

"I see a rainbow."

"Bring it up through the bottom of your feet, just like we did before, through every piece of your body, and push it out through the top of your head."

After an additional three minutes, I asked him to put the phone down and slowly walk around, taking what I like to call the walk of life, allowing his subtle energy field—his immune system—to re-balance and calibrate itself.

Afterwards, he told me his body felt light and fully flowing.

～

Using a very simple form of color, William was able to remove anger from his liver, and thereby remove the symptom. He continued his ColorWorks for another thirty days, even though he felt better; he had to reprogram his liver. I spoke to him eight years later, and though we'd worked just minutes on the telephone that day long ago, the pressure was still gone. He'd also learned how to express himself, and work in a more unconditional capacity. He was happy and content.

While this session was minor, others have been much more complex and yet have resulted in the same result. It's important to recognize that your body will literally and exactly do everything that you ask of it.

One of the greatest metaphysical metaphors states that we are body, mind, and spirit. I agree, but I disagree with the hierarchy.

According to traditional thought, your spirit is the most vital aspect, because it is your soul, your higher self. You are your spirit. Your mind is the second most important, because it allows you to make choices, to think, to discern, to identify, to comprehend, to reason. Your body is simply the vehicle which houses those two.

I like to think of it differently.

I agree that my spirit is the most important piece, but my body is a close second, because it is the vehicle in which the soul speaks to me. And the mind? It's the least important, for it allows me to fear. It tells me I'm not qualified, that I'm not capable, that something is out of my reach, out of my grasp, impossible. My body, though, will make literal truth out of everything I think and say. It doesn't have discernment.

We must be careful what we wish for. We'll always receive it, just rarely in the way we imagined.

5

EVERYONE LEARNS

FOR THE MOST PART, we create illness or disease ourselves, through use of our words and thoughts. But sometimes we can bring them into this life from our past life. I call these Karmic Lessons—lessons from a past life, a reincarnation, or as many scientists believe, a memory that is stored within our DNA from an ancestor.

It's important to understand that, while these are difficult for the child and/or parents, everyone learns a lesson. Grand-parents, siblings, aunts, uncles, nurses, doctors, etc.—all of us involved discover something new about ourselves.

~

Molly had an eight-year-old son, who we'll call Jeremy. He was a bright, engaging little boy who liked to play with G.I. Joes and Transformers, and before I spoke with his mother, she'd sent me pictures of him. He was younger in the images, but they showed a blonde-headed little rascal, with speckles of mud on his cheeks and a wide, life-loving grin plastered to his face. The hems of his pants were worn, the knees half-torn and ragged, and he was perched at the top of a Jungle Gym.

I think it's the smile I remember most.

As usual, I asked his mother to let me talk to him. She agreed, and I heard her say to him, "You're going to talk to Patti, now. Be good, and listen to what she has to say."

"Okay," he said, and there was a pause and a crackle as the phone changed hands.

Jeremy and I spoke a little to break the ice—what kinds of games he enjoyed, what his favorite television show was, what he wanted to be when he grew up—and then we got down to business. "So why did your mommy call me, Jeremy?"

In a very serious and articulate manner, he said, "I get lots of ear infections. My eusta . . . ." I heard his mother coaching him along. "My eustach . . . eustachian tubes are too narrow. They hurt, and I have to take lots of medicine. Yucky!"

I could hear the grimace in his voice, as he was suffering one right now, but there was also happiness in the tone, lightness, one that indicated he was happy simply to be alive, to love his mother, to experience the dirt on his palms and the mud on his pants.

Resisting the urge to laugh, I asked him to close his eyes, and suggested that he imagine all of his favorite colors were floating above his head. "What color do you need to make your Eustachian tubes wider?"

"Green and blue," he said with pride. "That's the colors of Captain Planet."

"Okay, imagine that green and blue are floating above your head, and imagine that they start shooting down beams of light into your ears. Can you see it?"

He giggled and said, "Yup."

This continued approximately four minutes, at which point I asked, "How do you feel? Do your ears still hurt?"

He was quiet for a moment, thinking. "Nope! Mom, my ears don't hurt anymore! See?" I could hear him moving the phone and tapping his ears, as if to prove to her that he was better. "Can I go back outside?"

~~

I learned a lot that day.

Sometimes we believe pain is necessary to heal. We often don't have the faith to believe miracles can happen in the blink of an eye. I realized that it wasn't whether or not I was qualified to work with a child, an adult, someone dying, or someone who just needed to learn different behaviors, and it wasn't because I was brilliant. Father had shown me my toolbox, one I could share and use with anyone, no matter their age or circumstance—a toolbox I've used every day of my life.

6

FEAR CREATES FEAR, CREATES DISEASE

I RUBBED THE SLEEP from my eyes, knowing the day wasn't quite done. My Wisconsin hotel room was sparse—a clean bed, a small desk and chair in the far corner, and an old television bolted to a heavy wooden frame. Brochures for the weekend's conference lay on the desk, their tri-fold pages spread out to display the back.

Someone tapped lightly on my door, and I opened it to allow my next appointment in. Her scooter buzzed through, past the bathroom, to the far wall and window, humming and squeaking slightly as she positioned it near the desk.

We'll call her Sylvia, and she simply looked at me, waiting. Her energy was beautiful, like a shard of sunshine piercing the clouds, or a flower that clung to life in the harshest desert.

I sat on the bedside, not wanting to brave the hard chair, and asked, "How can I help you?"

A tiny smile escaped, and she looked down at her scooter as if to say, "Can't you see?" Moments passed before she actually answered, and she did so timidly. "I've . . . I've been diagnosed with Multiple Sclerosis."

That's all she said, as if it would explain everything. Her desperation had driven her to silence, and she couldn't bring herself to speak of her illness. It ruled her, and her every motion struggled against it.

"Tell me about it." I knew this would be difficult, but also necessary. "Start slow, build your strength. Tell me about your life, your profession, your body. It's okay."

She placed her hands in her lap and lowered her head, but she spoke with more strength than before. "I'm a writer, and I'm working on a book about Catholic schools. I grew up in one not far from here. My parents only spoke to me about once every two months. It was . . . it was brutal. I suppose the nuns thought they were helping, that they were teaching us something, and I was never been sure if they knew how it affected the students. Would they have still done it, had they known? Would they—"

"Stop," I said, and placed a hand on her knee. "You don't have Multiple Sclerosis."

"What?" she replied, stunned. Then a subtle anger brewed beneath the surface. "I'm sitting in this damn scooter. I can barely walk, and three different doctors have all confirmed the diagnosis. Now you . . . you . . . want to tell me I don't have it?"

"This is what I think happened. You're writing a book based upon your life in a Catholic school system, right? And it includes what you perceived took place during those years. So, you started feeling numbness in your arms and legs, and you went to your physician. Right?"

She nodded.

"He's a good doctor, so he told you everything that might be wrong. He laid out all the scenarios, despite how terrible, or painful, or scary. In addition, he ordered a slew of tests according to your symptoms. He stated, quite calmly, that you could be experiencing symptoms of Multiple Sclerosis."

"He did. It was . . . it was terrifying." She glared down at her scooter as if cursing it. "I'd always been so secure in my health, in my body, but at that point, up was down. I was dizzy with it, so much that I couldn't think, couldn't feel. I'd stopped work on the book, and my sickness was all I could think about."

"But the first set of blood work was normal, wasn't it?" I didn't wait for her to say yes. "And so your doctor suggested an MRI to rule out Multiple Sclerosis. That type of fear is quite literally paralyzing, and when you finally had the test, it showed five lesions on your brain."

"Then how can you say it's not Multiple Sclero—"

"How many times did you fall down as a child?" I asked gently.

"I did a lot of gymnastics," she said as a way of explanation.

"Do you think it's at all possible that you hit your head hard enough to create lesions?"

"Of course."

"You don't have Multiple Sclerosis," I stated again. "The fear of that possibility created symptoms to concur with the diagnosis, but you don't actually *have* it. I need you to understand that your body doesn't have discernment capabilities, and, after you agonized so much about having this disease, your body said, 'I can do that.' Remember what Fear truly is; Forgetting Every Available Resource . . . forgetting all of the source and strength inside of you to remove your Multiple Sclerosis!"

≈

People with spinal cord injuries or Multiple Sclerosis often store rage or hatred in their spinal column, even though they're generally mild individuals. It's hard to make them angry, they are so laid back and mellow. Thus, Sylvia never got angry. She simply stewed, glaring down at her scooter, unwilling to say a bitter word. But unlike others who have the ability to vocalize their anger, she stored it deep. It burrowed within and created a serious illness.

When they do get angry, they explode. They get over it quickly, but typically with the thought process of, "I'll put it all behind me," and they store it directly into the vertebrae.

Sylvia illustrates how our bodies respond to spoken and unspoken words. They attach to emotions such as fear or rage, and they vibrate at a lower frequency than our bodies. They lodge in our cells and create blockages when triggered.

Disease takes place after a long series of logs in the river, and Sylvia's experiences at the Catholic school, and every moment of anger afterward, had slowly built her dam higher and higher. When she began to write her book, she remembered everything from her past, and her dam overflowed.

Can you change your life by changing what you say and think?

Absolutely!

Being aware of our language and emotional responses to what happens around us can prevent blockages in our bodies that can manifest later as disease. When we are in state of unconditional being, or unconditional love, our words vibrate at a higher frequency, and they don't cause blockages when stored in the body.

7

PERCEPTION IS EVERYTHING

GOD NEVER GAVE US a meaning, and there is no such thing as anger, love, jealousy, happiness, hatred, or joy. They're illusions. We created them to assign meaning to our lives, to make up a grand little story in our heads, at the time of any given event. They're words used to qualify what we are experiencing.

Take away our ability to speak, to think, and what if we were then to watch a sunrise—oranges splashed against a bluish-purple sky, with a hint of white to fray the edges. This sunrise is simply that: a sunrise. It's a natural event, prompted by natural forces, which produce a natural result. It's not positive, not negative; it's simply a sunrise.

Two different people will invariably see this differently. For me it is a stunning, gorgeous thing, and I may *ooh* and *ahh* and smile. For another, it may signify something far less appealing. It may be the day they bury their friend, and so that beauty is tinged with sadness. Not one soul will experience it exactly the way I do. Why? Because each of us clings to our own perception, according to our life experiences, and the vibration within ourselves.

David Eddings, in his fantasy series *The Belgariad*, writes, "The WORD determines the event. The WORD puts limits on the event and shapes it. Without the WORD, the event is merely a random happening."

Life is like that: it simply is. Our perception applies meaning—both positive and negative—to it, and our perception is our history. Our existence, our history, is defined by our words and emotions, and there is not one person that can make us feel loved, angry, or sad.

We choose it.

Resentment, rage, joy, pleasure—none of these actually exist. No emotions, good or bad, are real; they are just perceptions of an event, and when we allow ourselves the responsibility of our perception, we can go back through our lives and change them. An event that may have once been a challenge, such as burying that friend, can now be perceived differently. We are not changing the event itself, just the perception of the event, thereby changing our emotional reaction.

This is where it becomes oh-so-important: emotions we perceive as negative vibrate at a low frequency, and cause us to feel miserable or sick. But we must remember that no emotion is inherently positive or negative. Like everything else in the universe, it is just a frequency, and we can change our *perception* of these emotions, thus shifting the frequency.

We were born with everything needed to understand what the universe is saying, and what to do about it. Our perception determines what is stored in our bodies.

8

TRUTH AND HOW IT RELATES
TO PERCEPTION

SUPPOSE I WERE TO ask a group of people, "Why am I holding this cup of coffee?"

I would receive varied responses: "Because it's warm."; "Because you don't want it to spill."; "Because you like coffee."; or maybe, "Because you don't want to lose it."

The truth is that only I know the reason, and all other answers are simply perceptions. While each of us can give reasons—perceptions—of *why* I'm holding my coffee, I'm the only one who would truly know. Others don't have the same thoughts, the same history, the same perceptions as me.

Several years ago, I sat with my good friend, a Rabbi who had survived the Holocaust, and his best friend, a Catholic Priest. We'll call the Rabbi Levi, and we'll call the Priest George.

We sat in a historic tavern in upstate New York, with a thin haze of smoke to disguise the other patrons. Wind battered the old, cracked wooden door, and ancient, wavy glass panes revealed the world beyond as twisted and warped, depending on what angle one viewed them from.

33

Rabbi Levi, Father George, and I argued over one sentence of scripture for five hours:

Love is patient, love is kind.
—Corinthians 13:1

The details of this argument were not the important part. We were extremely vocal, never wavered, and passionately defended our beliefs.

Rabbi Levi and I had met years earlier, in a hospital after he'd experienced a heart attack, and instantly forged a friendship. So many stories he told me, but one stood out among the others.

I stood within a throng of men, half of them barely clothed, the other half clad in little more than rags. We were wretched things, living on uncooked tins of whatever the Germans gave us. I had a young friend in the camp, David, who was barely old enough to be considered a man—which wasn't much by the Nazi standards—and we shared a small corner of the bunker.

He came to me on that day, while we waited for the Germans to take us to the quarry, and asked, "What is the meaning of this, Levi? What's the point of it?"

And to that, I could only reply, "The point is the point. It's to show the rest of the world what they think we are, and also to show them what we think we are."

"And what are we?"

"We are love."

"And they?"

"Are also love."

Rabbi Levi's eyes glistened as he continued.

David died the next day, shot in the back by a guard who was convinced he wasn't working fast enough. I mourned for many, many years, and the only thing that kept me from the brink of madness was the memory of his smile. He understood. He forgave. And he loved.

Father George had a far different view of Corinthians 13:1. Many would say that his past wasn't as traumatic as Rabbi Levi's, but we must remember that perception is everything.

I was twenty-five when I entered the priesthood. I was twenty-six when I fell in love. However, we must remember that such a love is forbidden with my beliefs. I took an oath of celibacy, and thus I could never truly hold her.

To me, love is also sacrifice. Patience and kindness are elements, but it goes beyond that.

There was a moment of frustration, of intense anger, at the moment I told her I could never be with her. And then I had to let her go. I haven't seen her since that moment, not for an hour or a minute or a second, and I've missed her.

That is sacrifice. It is love.

Father George had spent his entire life coming to terms with his views of love, and how they had changed his life. His views weren't my views, as I didn't buy into the sacrifice angle as much, but I understood his point, and more than that, I understood what made him believe this way, what changed his *perception*.

Their truth was only their truth. Mine was different.

～

My big brother, David, was the bestest of all brothers. He taught me how to fish, how to gut said fish, and how to cook it in yummy juices of yumminess. He taught me how to run a trap line, how to snag our catch and prepare it to eat. Quicksand, with its grabby fingers, was no danger after he taught me how to recognize it. By the time I was five, I owned my own shotgun, and he showed me how to use it without injuring myself.

He was my hero.

When I was in my early 30s, he called and asked, "What do you remember about our childhood?"

"It was growing up with you, fishing, learning how to hunt, how to survive in the wilderness."

I was so excited to share these memories with him, and yet there was total silence on the other end of the phone.

"What?"

In a very quiet voice, he said, "Those were the worst years of my life. I wasn't allowed to leave the house without taking you with me, and I just wanted to be alone."

To me, he'd been my knight in shining armor. To him, I'd been the bane of his existence. Yet he never took it out on me. He was never cruel, and always treated me with never-ending patience.

Looking back, I could understand how he may have been exasperated as I watched trees speaking to each other, or listened to a rock for hours, all the while being aware that he stood, watching, patiently waiting for me to finish.

When we view our lives, we must also look at how much chaos we create when we feel the need to be right. If we can acknowledge and accept that our opinions are only truth for us, then we can ease the frustration of when others don't see the world as we do.

Even now, as you read the words in the story above, their meaning will be determined by your perception. It's not because they are unclear, but because you didn't write them. You may have an idea of what I mean, but that's ultimately a guess.

In the case of myself, Father George, and Rabbi Levi, we merely expressed our beliefs—our *perceptions*—as they pertained to love. I explained the love of my brother. Rabbi Levi explained the love of a friend, and what that meant to him, and Father George told us his perspective on a love that was never meant to be.

None of us was wrong. Perceptions are based off our histories, and because we're the only ones that experienced that *exact* history, no one else can hold the same perception.

9

REACTIONS, JUDGMENT AND
DISCERNMENT, LIFE AND LIMITS

Reactions

Consider this: if someone spits in your face—a big, sloppy clam—will you be angry?

My answer is: I can choose my reaction. I can choose to be angry and yell at him. However, that anger will be stored in my body. I, not he, will be harmed by my outburst.

Am I saying that what he did was right? No. I'm saying that I have not lived his history, nor do I have his perceptions. I don't know *why* he did what he did; I know only that he did it.

Again, it's my choice. I can choose outraged indignation, or I can choose a path of Unconditional Love. I can say, "Thank you, I have not had a shower today." On the other hand, I can say, "Thank you. Did that make you feel better?" Whether I choose to be angry or an observer determines what vibrational energy I put into my body.

Thus, my *reaction* is far more important than his *action*.

As we go through life, many of us begin to comprehend that there is no right or wrong. Things simply are.

Judgment or Discernment

Individual experiences grant us our perceptions, which in turn present us with another choice: judgment or discernment. Being able to tell the difference between the two is essential in maintaining a healthy energetic vibration in our bodies.

Judgment is a perception with an emotion attached to it. If I were to get angry with a man spitting in my face, that is judgment. If I notice someone wearing dirty clothes, and think that mine are cleaner, and therefore better, that is a judgment. The more I can stay out of judgment, the less low vibration energies are stored in my body.

Discernment is a perception with *no* emotion attached to it. It is looking at someone who spits in my face and thinking, "That is the path of his soul, and I respect it." Discernment is recognizing when someone's purpose or truth is different from mine. If it is unpleasant, such as the spitting, I can still honor that soul and its path, even if next time I cross the street to avoid him.

When attempting to remain out of judgment, it helps me to truly understand that God is in charge, and that events will unfold in the time and place that He accords. The more peaceful and calm we can look at our lives, the better we can make choices that keep us free from judgment.

After all, it can be easy to blame or judge when things go awry. However, we *chose* to engage in the situation.

Ask yourself, "What is it I need to learn? What do I need to discern from this situation? How can I stay out of judgment?"

Each of us must look at who we are now as individuals, and look back at our past in an effort to recognize how we were raised, understand what we've learned, and apply those dynamics to ourselves as we are now.

We always have choice. We always have options.

We have the ability to look back at our lifetime; deal with whatever it is we need to look at either in psychotherapy or in deep meditation. The most important thing to get out of this, however, is an understanding of how you grew.

What was the positive learning lesson that became part of you during your time of stress? Duality must exist—for every negative there is a positive. Look back at your life and see the negatives, but find the positives and allow *that* to become your focus.

You can't change your parents; you can't change your siblings. These are wonderful mirrors for you to look at, and decide whether or not their behavior is what you want in your life. If it's not one that you'd like to continue, then it is your responsibility to change behavior and lead a different life.

You can accept your parents and siblings for who they are, the beautiful souls that have come into this lifetime to help teach. Remember, however, that you can respect them for who they are, and yet walk a different path.

An important aspect of life is being able to look at our loved ones with discernment, not judgment. Love them for who they are, but understand when your lessons are learned; you're now ready to move on to your next adventure.

Life is Perfect

All of the great Masters—Jesus, Buddha, Shiva, Abraham, and Mohammed, to name a few—have delivered a similar message: spirituality is the practice of Unconditional Being.

Also called Unconditional Love, Unconditional Being is the ability to accept that all is perfect, just the way it is, even if something does not make sense intellectually, or seems cruel or unfair. It is the ability to suspend judgment.

Truly, we do not need to judge.

Why?

Because life is perfect. *We* are perfect. How can we make mistakes when there is no right or wrong? We cannot. With each breath, we learn. When we suspend our judgments, we discern the lessons to be learned without recording low vibrations in our bodies.

When we stay in balance in our lives, we have simplicity at all levels.

No Limits

A psychologist friend once said to me, "What you don't get is that you have limitations."

"You're right," I said. "I don't."

"You don't get it?"

"No, I mean I don't have limitations. People do not have limitations."

Limitations are perceptions we impose on ourselves, and not something inherently human. Yes, we do have physical limitations, but we can overcome many obstacles by not looking at life as an obstacle.

Remember, if you perceive a wall, then a wall is what you will get. However, if you change your perception of a wall and look at it as a stair, then you can create the next step in your life.

Setting goals is important because we are survivalists and achievers.

I can be an astrophysicist. Why? Because that's where my true passion lies. I could fling numbers and theories around, splattering them against the wall like dabs of paint. Setting a goal in alignment with passion allows me to be successful.

Don't tell yourself you're not qualified. Instead, look at life and know that you're qualified and able, and then look at what you are truly passionate about. Move forward from there. You may not achieve your goal in this lifetime, but you *will* achieve it—in God's time, not your time.

Mind, Body, Spirit, and Limits

As I mentioned in Chapter 4, each of us is body, mind, and spirit, and of the three, it is our minds that can limit us.

While the spirit is indeed most important, it's our *bodies* that communicate messages from Source, because our bodies are solid, substantial forms that only relay truth. The more we listen to them, the better we accurately understand what's happening in our lives.

When we try to use our minds to decipher messages, we limit ourselves. We doubt the accuracy of the messages, even though they are always the truth. We second guess ourselves, and can feel confused, or maybe we interpret it based upon the history of what we already know. Therefore, we aren't open to every possibility, especially those we haven't experienced yet.

My belief is that illness and pain are ways our bodies get the message across. We live at such a low vibration; it's the only way our bodies can get our attention. It's the only way we understand, and nothing happens by accident, not even the most insubstantial bruise. When we listen to the small clues—maybe a minor headache, dizziness, or perhaps a weakness of the muscles—and then *trust* those clues, we may not need to experience severe disease or pain.

Pay attention to what your body says, but, more than that, learn to trust it.

We often fear what could happen to us, rather than listening to the message our bodies are telling us.

Take this example: when a child falls and skins his knee, a parent may rush to him, creating emotional drama to go along with the event itself. A well-intentioned parent may say, "We'd better get that cleaned up or it might get infected."

His body senses the parent's fear, and he only hears, "It will get infected." So his body responds with, "I can do that." He's learning to fear what could happen to him, instead of listening to and trusting his body. It also begins a pattern that if his body hurts, then it could be life threatening or serious.

Instead, if the parent calmly says, "Let's go get that cleaned up. What can I do so that you are feeling more supported?" Then he is able to think about what has happened, listen to his body, and respond with what he needs. It could be as easy as working on his balance, or strengthening his legs. Or it could go deeper than the physical, and into the mental, such as becoming surer of himself.

A child does not fall for just any reason at all. Nothing happens by accident. It's simply his body attempting to convey a message.

10

S.H.I.T. (SPIRITUAL HUMAN IN TRANSITION)

DAY ONE: A BIRD tweets, the flowers are blooming on your rose bush next to the house, and your new job starts tomorrow. Everything is perfect, dandy, couldn't be better.

Day Two: The cat dragged in the bird's carcass, the flowers wilted and dried up, turning a crusty reddish color, and your new job just became your old job. Everything is wrong, terrible, couldn't be worse.

That's growth, and it's what I call the S.H.I.T. effect. We don't grow when we are happy, when the flowers are blooming and the birds are tweeting. We don't grow when the bills are paid, when we can float in our pool and drink margaritas, with no responsibilities to bring us down.

While some of the above scenario might sound great, eventually we get bored. We aren't pushing ourselves to search out, to create growth in our souls.

When S.H.I.T. happens, we grow.

≈

On a beautiful summer's day, the sun was shining so brightly, and peacefulness surrounded me, only to be disturbed by the screech of my telephone.

A man clearly in distress said, "I need to have an appointment. I need to talk to you. Today. Now."

Now wasn't an option, and so we made arrangements for the following day, at which time I asked him, "What's happening in your life personally, professionally, and physically?"

Professionally, he'd once worked a good job, an upper-level management position for a respected company. He'd been there for ten years before they let him go. But that was then, and this was now.

House: lost.

Car: lost.

Life savings: lost.

Physically, he was a wreck.

And the root of it all was personal.

He spoke haltingly. "My wife divorced me four years ago—one of the most painful experiences I've ever experienced."

He fell silent, and I said, "And?" as a way to prompt him.

"So I began rebuilding my life, putting one step in front of the other, beginning work again at the local supermarket. What else is there to do, right?" he said with a sarcastic laugh. "My wife and I, we shared custody of our son, who was only twelve at the time we divorced. I saw him as much as I could—baseball games, picking him up after school for Oreo-sprinkled ice cream, playing with remote-controlled cars as the sun drifted down at my apartment."

"And?"

"And that was it. The sun drifted down."

"There must be more than—"

"Two years after the divorce, he was diagnosed with leukemia. Nothing in my life—not losing my wife, not losing my job, or my house, or my car—compared to watching him go through chemotherapy and radiation, knowing his body was still deteriorating." His voice broke, but he forced himself to continue. "Within a year, my son passed away. Everything in my life had dissolved."

"You've really been through shit."

"Ma'am, my life has fallen apart."

"No," I said gently. "You're truly in S.H.I.T."

⁓

A Spiritual Human in Transition—it's when our life totally falls apart, and we wonder how we'll get the strength to make it another day. This is when we are in growth.

It was at first challenging to find the good in what this man had gone through, but he went through it for a reason. Even though we may not always see the big picture, we must take solace in knowing that everything happens for a reason. In the months following his son's passing, we worked with positive perception, applying it to what had happened.

One might ask, "What could possibly be positive in all of this?"

That's easy, but painful. He finally understood people, their suffering, and their joy. "Ma'am," he once told me, "I realized that for most of my life, I never cared about other people, their feelings, or their hardships. I'd been selfish, selfish."

Through all of that, through all the S.H.I.T., he'd mucked through, he'd grown into an incredibly caring man who not only cared for himself, but gave to others as well. He'd found a better job, and yet still donated much of his check to those in need. He'd come through with a personality and essence that I found beautiful.

What a gift his son had given him: to live, to experience.

Things such as life traumas, unemployment, illness, heartache, and family relationships force us to look deeply within ourselves in an attempt to change our lives. Because the pain is greater than staying where we are . . . we change. We grow. We evolve.

People usually experience pain in one of two situations: a health crisis, or a relationship crisis. These are the two most powerful mechanisms God uses to get our attention, and thus allows us to grow.

As we touched on in Chapter 9, disease or injury is simply a way our bodies talk to us, providing the opportunity to re-evaluate our lives and how we have conducted ourselves, thereby affording the potential for tremendous growth.

Relationships, on the other hand, also offer great opportunity for growth, as they affect us emotionally, and potentially physically. Let us first look at relationships and how they affect our day-to-day lives.

Love is emotional, not logical.

When we fall in love, we are planted firmly in emotion. Our hearts flutter at the sight of our significant others, and we can't help but wish to be with them. It's something without reason, and cannot be rationalized.

At some point, however, it becomes logical. What was once an unreasoning urge is now a question: "Can I make time to see this person today? Golly, I'm not sure. I've got to feed my turtle, and water my plants, and I've really got to do something about that rusty hinge. I'll see them Saturday, anyways."

That's a classic case of logical love, and in so many instances that is where it stays. The love is undeniably there, as we would be heartbroken to never see that person again, but it has become logical and practical. Our relationship becomes a give-and-take, whereas before it was neither. It simply burned. In order for a relationship to truly last, to be in balance and a true blessing, it must be a combination of both emotion and logic.

But how do we do that? Where's the balance, and at what point do the scales tip too far in one direction? As we experience the logical love, we must look at certain dynamics: do we live in the same geographical location? Do we have the same sleeping habits? Do we have sexual compatibility? Is our financial situation compatible? All of these components are important to the sustainability of a relationship. That's the meat and potatoes of it, the yum-yums that we deal with daily.

But we *do* fall in love—the unexplainable, irresistible sensation—and that's emotional. When we look in each other's eyes, we experience recognition, a desire, a need, an understanding that truly transcends logical thought. As we experience emotional love, we must again look at certain dynamics: is it *too* irresistible? Has logic permanently flown the way of the cuckoo? And, perhaps most importantly, is it a balanced love, or is one person much deeper than the other?

Like everything else, love—both logical and emotional—must be balanced.

It's important within any relationship to know yourself as well as you possibly can. Understand what your boundaries are in terms of who you are as a person. What are you willing to accept from a spouse? What is your personal moral and ethical stance on a relationship? For some people, infidelity is grounds to end a relationship. For others, infidelity is grounds for discussion, not termination. For some, dishonesty, gambling, and financial instability are reason enough to terminate a relationship.

The better you know yourself, the greater chance you have for a successful relationship. If you don't know your own boundaries, how can you possibly expect your partner to know what you expect from the relationship?

When we enter a relationship (other than in arranged marriages), we do so with our heart, not with our minds. Anytime we approach something with our hearts open, we will perceive the most accurate truth. It is only when we are vulnerable that we learn the most. We can learn with our minds, but we learn faster through our heart.

There are no mistakes. Everything is perfect in terms of your spiritual existence. The key to peace is to incorporate a belief that it is okay not to know why something happens, or why someone has behaved in a way that upset you. You can't change someone else! It doesn't matter what role you play. The important aspect is to look at your life and see if it fits with your moral and ethical beliefs.

Are your personal boundaries being respected? Is your partner treating you in accordance with the boundaries that you have established? If not, love yourself enough to discuss the issue with your partner, work towards resolution, change your thoughts, or simply accept that your partner is not compatible at this stage in your life.

Love Conquers All

So many of us believe love conquers all of our challenges. We hear it so often. But, for most of us, love only conquers for a short time, until logic once again raises its somewhat ugly head to gobble up touchy-feely emotion.

For example: many relationships function incredibly well until children come into the picture. Children can cause incredible stress within the relationship itself, which, for the most part, is then functioning almost entirely on a logical level. As soon as emotions such as resentment, bitterness, or anger appear, it becomes challenging for two individuals to overcome them without professional help.

In some cases, it's time for these two people to move on. They've experienced what they needed to, or they've had the children they needed to have. There's nothing to be ashamed of in this instance.

While we often take vows *for better or for worse*, those weren't intended to cause misery over an extended period of time. If a woman is married to a man who emotionally abuses her and physically beats her, should she stay within the relationship because it's *for worse*?

Of course not.

If a man finds out that is wife has been unfaithful and she is unwilling to change behavior or commit to counseling, does he stay in the marriage because it's *for worse*?

Certainly not.

However, it's difficult for most people to find and accept a balance. It's perhaps impulsive to dissolve a relationship when issues are first raised, and we need to be reasonable. We should all ask ourselves questions:

1. How is it affecting you emotionally?

2. Have you attempted to work it out?

3. Have you sought professional counseling?

4. If there are children, how is the situation affecting them?

5. Have each of you faithfully worked to understand each other's needs?

If the answer to all of those are "Yes," and you are still experiencing resentment and bitterness because your needs are not being met, then it's time to look at the possibility of leaving, or having a professional regression to see if the cause can be identified.

Most of all, it's important to act, to look at your own behavior. You can't change your partners, you can only change yourself. And if circumstances can't be changed, then you must accept that your partner is no longer part of your path.

Does that mean that there is something wrong with them? Absolutely not. It simply means that you've grown in different directions, that you've become different people who no longer look at life the same way. It's simply a matter of incompatibility, and most professional marriage counselors will tell you, "The worst thing about a bad marriage is staying one day longer than necessary."

More than the logical and emotional aspects of a relationship, let's look at how they affect our bodies.

Carol first called me on a Wednesday in the middle of December. A white sheen of frost glistened beyond my office window, and the low hum of my heater filled the room. We began the appointment with my customary question: tell me about your life personally, professionally, and physically.

Her voice was loud, boisterous, with a bitter edge that pierced the speaker. "I'm in a very challenging relationship. It wasn't that way before, but, well, now it is."

As if that explained anything.

"Children?" I asked.

"No."

"Financial problems?"

"I don't. He does."

"Then let's start there and—"

"No, that's not what I wanted to talk about. Every time we have sex, I get an infection. A bad infection. I don't want to have sex with *him* anymore, but I'm concerned he'll step out on me."

And then she ranted, and ranted, and ranted. No expense was spared, so to say, and she touched more on sex, and then on love, history, money, her work as an actress—anything that popped into her head.

So I listened, and at the end of it I asked, "So, about the financial problems."

"That's not what I wanted to—"

"You don't currently work, and neither does he. How do you think that may be affecting your relationship?"

"Well, I . . . well, I expect him to provide for me. He hasn't had a job for a month. A month! And the lazy S.O.B. hasn't gotten one in all that time. He should provide for me, right? That's how it works, right?"

I said the next part delicately. "Do you think you're being a little passive aggressive here?"

"I . . . well, maybe."

Clearly, the stress of their finances, and the resentment and bitterness that she now felt, was triggering an allergic reaction. However, this wasn't an allergy to pollen, or fish, or bees. It was an allergy to him. The issue was not an allergy; it was bitterness and resentment.

Carol and I began the process of ColorWorks, in which we asked her body, "What color do I need to remove my bitterness and resentment?" For the next ten minutes she moved whatever color she perceived, bringing it into her body from the bottom of her feet, up her legs, and out her mouth, but I wasn't entirely happy with what I was seeing. It was clear that we needed to get her boyfriend on the phone, to begin discussion on expectation and needs within their relationship.

During our next session, both Carol and David were on the phone, and he expressed his own resentment at her expectation that he provide the finances. "It's not fair. She hasn't worked in months either. My father died very early, working extremely hard in an attempt to provide for an unhappy wife. I see that here, now, being repeated. I don't want to die young or unhappy."

They were both silent for a moment, and then Carol said, "I knew that, I just . . . well, I never put everything together. Not until now."

Their homework assignment was for each of them to utilize ColorWorks for removing bitterness and resentment, and to individually list their expectation and needs within the relationship.

I am happy to say that they were able to work through their challenges. After thirty days using ColorWorks, they both had much less bitterness and resentment, and they'd taken my suggestion about therapy. She'd actively sought out a part-time position, which gave her some financial freedom, and gave David the support he needed not to feel fully financially responsible.

Communication

I think John Gray was correct when he said, "Men are from Mars, and women are from Venus."

Sometimes the actions of other people, especially those of the opposite sex, are exasperating and difficult. We often get upset and ask, "Why do they act that way? It really hurts my feelings!"

The fact of the matter is that we will never know exactly *why* they forget to take out the trash, or leave their makeup sprawled across three bathrooms, or plop their dirty dishes on the counter, or stick long, long strands of hair to the shower walls, or seem to purposely miss the clothes hamper. We only know that they do, and sometimes they may not even know why.

This is why communication is so important. Dialogue is necessary to understand—to the best of our ability—*why* our partners act the way they do.

And it goes beyond the everyday routines. A man may ask, "Why does she need to discuss everything?" On the other hand, a woman may say, "He never discusses how he feels."

Think back to caveman times—the men continually hunted. The women, however, raised the young, prepared the food, sewed the clothes, tended the fire, and nurtured her family. They focused on different things, and their brains developed differently.

When I look at a man's brain physiology, in 98% of the cases, he will be functioning from one quadrant. When I look at a woman's brain physiology, in 98% of the cases, she functions out of two or more quadrants at any given time. Women have evolved into multitaskers.

Here's another example: have you ever observed a man when he's on the telephone? If his partner comes up to him and says, "Honey, what would you like for dinner?" The man will *typically* say, "Shh! Can't you see I'm on the phone?"

A woman can be on the phone, ironing clothes, with a child at her feet, and still know everything that's taking place. Women are much better at multitasking, whereby men are focused and intent upon the current task.

We think differently. And before we feel as though our partners are not hearing us, or are not considerate of us, we must look at how we communicate.

At the heart of everything, we see, hear, feel, taste and smell. All of us communicate using one of those senses. For example, some of us respond best to the spoken word—we're auditory. Others respond best with a note left on the fridge— they're visual. Rarely do we feel messages, and even rarer yet is the taste or smell form of communication.

What's important to note is that, over time, we may shift in how we communicate. The man who once responded best to the note on the fridge may not even notice it now. He may need to be told.

It goes beyond that, into how we actually *ask* our questions. For example, a man may say, "Honey, did you see that?" Through twenty years of marriage, his wife has always responded, but now she may just ignore the question—not because she doesn't want to answer it, but because it's no longer phrased correctly. Her communication pattern is now be auditory, and if she asked the same question but using the terminology of, "Honey, did you *hear* that?" she will in all probability answer the question.

From time to time, we all need to listen to *how* our partners are speaking. Are they saying, "I hear that," or, "I see that," or, "I feel that?" These are all indicators of how your partner is now communicating.

I once dated a man who had teenaged children. It was very interesting to watch the dynamic between father and children.

One son, the father perceived, was unusually rebellious. As his son would leave the house on a weekend evening, he would always say, "Be home by eleven."

Yeah, that never happened. His son never responded and simply left, never arriving home by the prescribed time.

After observing this for many months, I realized the father didn't understand he and his son were communicating incorrectly. I gently suggested that he was auditory, while his son was visual. Moreover, if he truly wanted to end the conflict, he would simply post on the door the guidelines of when his son needed to be home.

He did, and his son was.

Why invest emotional strength and energy to delve into *why* a loved one acts or feels a certain way, when you will never know exactly their thought pattern or feeling? This goes back to Chapter 8, and all of these topics are related.

Perception is everything—perception of behavior, perception of response, perception of response to the response to the behavior, and so on. We cannot change someone else's actual behavior, but we can change our perception of it.

11

LIVE IT, DON'T WISH IT!

LIKE A SORE THROAT, if something is upsetting or affecting us physically, it is the universe sending us information about our behavior. We can either be caught up in acting the part of victim or martyr, or we can give thanks to the situation and ask ourselves, "What is God telling me? What do I need to learn? *Have* I learned?"

Then—and this is the kicker—we need to actually *listen*, not with our brains, but with our hearts and bodies.

As with injury and illness, everything happens for a reason. Believing an experience is right or wrong is simply a way of compartmentalizing life, throwing unnecessary labels on things, and it ensures you *will* encounter the learning experience again! That's what experiences are: opportunities to learn. And if we don't learn what we're supposed to, guess what? We flunk the test and start over.

We experience marriages, divorces and reconciliations, and we suffer diseases, injuries and doubts. Yet we suffer less when we understand that these things have served a purpose, and then let it go and move on.

When relationships break down or disease enters our lives, we feel as though our world is falling apart. There's not much to do about it except to accept and learn. The universe does not care who we are or what we do. We will go through rough times, and we will grow, just like everybody else. No exceptions.

Still, it's always amazing to see individuals who are facing a terminal illness, and yet their strength wells and shines like a beacon for all to witness.

≈

Rural Kentucky, where Bradley and his parents lived, was reminiscent of an early 1900s village. An old, cracked sign swung on rusty hinges over the local saloon, and a large wooden porch covered the front of each home. They had picket fences, but the posts were green and moldy, the cross-bars crumbling and rotten.

Bradley's house, located twenty miles from the nearest town, was no different. Their piecemeal mailbox, half metal and half wood, sat alongside the deep ruts that stretched from the road to their driveway.

Once a year, my then husband Charlie Brown and I would brave that driveway to take Bradley and his parents on a shopping spree, and eat some great squirrel stew with just a hint of moonshine to spice the sauce.

Bradley, now almost twelve years old, didn't have any hair—chemotherapy and radiation had seared it away. His arms were bright and pasty, and the sunlight caused him pain, as he squinted even in the dimmest of lights. His cancer had been in remission for an entire year, and he'd spent that time with his family and friends, doing all the things every boy of his age does, but now it was back again to destroy his body.

"I don't want to take the drugs again," he said quietly, as we all sat around the table. Then he said it stronger. "I won't take them again."

His mother hung her head. "But—"

"If this is what God wants, then we need to listen. He don't make mistakes, Mama, and if this is what He wants, then it's what I want too."

His parents were devastated, but stood brave and respected his wishes, young as he was.

During the next six months, Bradley's body continued deteriorating, but his enthusiasm for life remained joyful and strong. His friends from school, and his minister from church, came over to his house often to visit and help keep his spirits raised.

One day, Bradley called me and told me he wanted to talk about God. I chuckled, as he was also close with his minister, and we often talked about Jesus, but he wanted to know something specific.

"Patti, my minister says Jesus will come for me when I die."

"Yes," I replied. "What was the question?"

"You always talk about God, but not so much Jesus. Why is that?"

"Bradley, God has always been the center of my life, and is the father of Jesus, but Jesus also is important to me. I believe that whomever we have a wish for, a desire for, a belief in, will be there for us as we die."

"Hmm, do you suppose that God could come get me? I think I'd really like it to be Him. That would make me feel even better."

I laughed and said, "You know, Bradley, all we can do is ask."
And so we prayed.

Six days later we received a phone call from Bradley's mother, and she told us he had passed in the early hours of the morning. She told me that for a while, as he got closer to death, she became scared. He would sit straight up in bed, even though he hadn't been able to sit up for the past three weeks, and his eyes would be as wide as they'd go, staring around the room.

She'd asked him if the Angels had come, and he replied, "No, Mama, it's not Angels."

"Bradley, has Jesus come for you?"

"No, Mama, it's not Jesus."

"And my heart thumped and thumped as I looked around and asked him, 'Bradley, if it's not Jesus, who's here?' And you know what, Patti? His eyes just twinkled the brightest I've ever seen them, and he smiled the widest I've ever remembered, and he said, 'Mama, tell Patti that God has come for me Himself!'"

His mother softly, and with a loving caress, instructed Bradley to lie back down and to go with God. Which he did. With a smile on his face.

At Bradley's memorial service, the whole town that he had spent his twelve years in closed down, and virtually everyone stopped to honor this young man and his courage.

≈

Bradley had a ripple affect not only on his family's lives, but on hundreds of people who knew him, and he was instrumental in the soul progression of people who probably never recognized how much he had touched their lives.

When we see those we love facing an illness or disease, it can hurt us, and sometimes we feel as though our own hearts are being ripped out. The more you can understand, no matter how painful, that this experience will ultimately assist others, the more you'll help them achieve growth and a continued soul progression.

We, as individuals, are not here to save the world, our families, or our friends. Other's lives and experiences are not ours to fix, and this is often a tremendous re-education for many people.

As soon as you decide to fix something, you will find yourself in deep S.H.I.T., because you are in the most human form of judgment. Our only job is to remain in our own honesty and integrity, to be out of judgment and ego.

Our work on this Earth is determined by how we conduct our lives on a day-to-day basis. The end of the journey is *not* what is recalled, but how we walked the path.

A Sacred Space

Understand that life is about flowing, not fixing. What we do has everything to do with who we are as a soul. The more we can stay in a place of Unconditional Love, without the intent to fix, the more other souls can choose whether or not to engage.

Many people believe that, as they incorporate an unconditional approach, they will surround themselves with like-minded people. Life will be serene and harmonious.

This is not the case.

Be prepared to encounter even greater obstacles and challenges. If you have walls up, protecting a sacred space, understand that something will make you vulnerable, crash down those walls, and make you more receptive to learning.

As souls, we are here to learn. Period. A soul can make a decision that, with human thought, can be deemed as good or bad, although it needn't be viewed as either. We souls are not emotionally perfect, or we would not be here again in human form. Thus we must perceive our experiences as learning opportunities.

In the last fifteen years, research in cellular vibration tells us that the cells of our bodies have two modes of operation: protection and growth. The cell is always in one of these two modes. On one hand, our cells must grow to ensure the integrity and continuous regeneration of our bodies. On the flip side, if our cells are in protection mode, it's likely because we are in a state of conditionality, or hiding to avoid chaos or pain.

Be mindful of this, for there will be a learning experience in the near future.

You must be aware of your Sacred Space, of holding onto your positive, sacred energy. It's simple: positive always comes from a negative. Duality must exist. For example: look at every major event that has taken place—earthquakes, volcanoes, wars, etc. Each of them was deemed tragic, but good eventually came out of it. People come together to help each other during catastrophes.

I always remember September 11th, 2001, when I think of this. Being from upstate New York, I have many happy memories of New York City.

As I sat stunned and watched on TV as those planes hit the Twin Towers, I couldn't even begin to fathom a terrorist attack. While I have traveled to many hot spots in the world, I'd never expected my own country to become a target.

But, watching the days that followed, the good from this event was clear. People actually spoke to each other. They were courteous, and horns weren't honking in traffic. We had developed an acceptance within the races that we, unfortunately, don't normally see in this country.

A week after 9/11, I was lecturing at the Mile High Church in Denver Colorado. I told the audience, "The one thing that will make me sad is if we all go back to where we were before last week. We were angry, judgmental, contrary, and mean-spirited."

In many ways, we've begun to take steps beyond that behavior, and yet, sadly, it is still all too pervasive.

Just remember these few things:

1. Life is only as difficult as you perceive it to be.

2. Validate your feelings without bringing judgment into your body. We are tiny, but not insignificant.

3. In the journey of life, it matters not where we go, but how we get there.

4. Take responsibility for your words and perceptions, and watch your soul grow.

12

INTUITION IS NOT A
TWELVE-STEP PROGRAM

First, let me say I truly believe all of us were born with exactly the same amount of intuition. It's quite simple, really: there is nothing I can do that you can't. It all comes down to trust. Trust in your body, trust in your thoughts, trust in your soul.

Intuition is the fine-tuning and compilation of all five of our senses.

It's is trusting that everything we sense is truth. You *can't* make a mistake. Absolutely trust what you know. How? Well, that's easy: simply keep in mind that you already know all of this; you're just remembering. My belief is that we're born fully sighted and fully knowing. We forget. How do we learn to incorporate this knowledge into our lives?

My son, Daniel, was struggling with a problem as a teenager, and he became upset as I was trying to comfort him. "You know," he said, "you really are arrogant."

"Excuse me?"

"God speaks directly to you. The rest of us have to figure it out, and it's not easy."

Well, yes and no. I walk in my right brain, or intuition, but I'm an analytical person. I have to understand it. In addition to that—and the truly important bit—God speaks directly to us all. He is our intuition. We just need to trust and listen.

1. Step 1: There is no Step 1.
2. Step 2: Refer to Step 1.

I do everything Father tells me as soon as it's said, but that doesn't mean I don't sit and analyze it for three days. For example, at age 12, a teacher told me I reminded her of Edgar Cayce, so, like any good teacher would do, she sent me to the store to buy his book.

I reached for it on the top shelf, and my arm froze above my head. I couldn't move, and Father's voice rumbled in my mind. "Stop. Do *not* contaminate the knowledge and information you have within. That is yours, and yours alone."

At that, I grimaced. "Okay, fine, just let me have my arm back."

Carpel Tunnel Nurse

A nurse came to me with carpal tunnel syndrome. She scheduled the appointment on Monday, needed to see me by Tuesday, and walked away without pain. This is how it happened.

I asked her, "What is your body telling you?"

"Nothing," she answered, but I could see the words circling around her head. "Nothing at all."

"What do you hear?" I asked.

"Nothing," she said. "I'm fine."

And so we danced. I asked her a question, and she dodged it. I pressured her, and she put up a shield. It went around like this for a few minutes, and then I said, "That's not true. Tell me what you hear."

She looked at me, exasperated. "Fine. All I hear is a stupid song from the '70s. It goes, 'You don't have to be a star.'" She paused, and her eyes widened slightly. "Oh, I get it!"

I explained why. "You've put so much pressure on yourself to be perfect, as many of our lives depend upon our performance. You have to be the star, and you stored that pressure in your wrist."

"There's more, isn't there?" she asked, sensing what was coming next.

"If I ask you how you are, and the answer is 'fine,' it simply means you're not willing to tell me how you're feeling. In my line of work, fine stands for Fearfully Internalizing Necessary Events. It means you're scared, and you don't want to go there."

<hr>

When we first learn to apply our intuition in helping others, we just remember that everyone has blockages. It's natural, and it's nothing to be ashamed of. For those of you looking to assist others, keep in mind that the difference between an intuitive and a good intuitive is not limiting yourself to one or two senses.

1. See.
2. Taste.
3. Smell.
4. Touch.
5. Listen.

Imagine that we stand in the middle of a forest. A birch tree sways to the left, its branches cracking and snapping with each gust of wind. The air smells damp from the morning's dew, with a faint tinge of mold. And the taste of it . . . the taste of this day is one of freshness, like a bite of a recently plucked orange.

And then? Then we intuit.

So we've established intuition, what it is, and how to interpret it, but it's important to be aware that the things we intuit are not always what we think they'll be.

For example, since the time God slapped my hand for attempting to grab an Edgar Cayce book, I haven't been allowed to read or study other individuals' work.

So, many years later, what did my intuition—God—tell me? Ah, yes, of course. It's time to study hypnotherapy. I had no idea what it was, really, and the little I did know wasn't terribly positive. It was mind control, or so I thought.

I wasn't ready or prepared to study this thing, but I did, because that's what my intuition told me to do. And I realized my earlier assumptions couldn't have been further from the truth. After two days of training, I learned hypnotherapy was just a continuation, another expansion, of my ability to understand my mind.

Tips for practitioners and patients:

1. It isn't enough to analytically understand the changes we need to make. Our changes must go deeper, and psychological therapy helps us deal with the mental or emotional part of an event. However, if the energy remains in our bodies, we are destined to repeat our behavior.

2. Because behavioral change is the goal, don't work on people who don't know they're being worked on.

3. Don't remove one hundred percent of an energy blockage from someone's body. They need to do the ColorWorks homework in order to take responsibility and change their own behavior.

4. If there is no change in the way a person is speaking or perceiving her life, she will simply continue to create her disease.

5. *You* are responsible for everything you say. That can't be emphasized enough.

The Soul Path and Intuition

Every soul is here to do something, whether that's to evolve, to rest, or on rare occasions, simply to exist. We started to die the moment the sperm entered the egg. Not born, but conceived. We are all going to die. It's inevitable.

We must let go of this fear of death, as it's simply a change of form, a progression of our soul's path, and that's all. However, we can't check out until we've accomplished our job in this life.

For me, I explain free will as follows: "You can be happy or miserable, but you *will* walk the path that you and the Universe agreed upon before you entered this physical form."

There's a strange disconnect there, between free will and the soul path. The soul path almost seems to imply that there's no such thing as free will, but that's not what I believe. We have a path, we have a goal, but how we get there is up to us.

People often ask me, "How do I know if I'm on the path?"

I answer, "How can you possibly be *off* the path?"

Few people know what their path is, but think about this: if we don't know what our path is, then we can't be off it. Because, there isn't just one soul path, there are thousands. As long as we reach the end goal, the place that we and God agreed upon before we entered this world, then we're right where we need to be.

That's where perception comes into play.

We can be happy or sad, but at the end of our lives, we *will* have accomplished what we needed to accomplish. We're always on path, always on purpose. If we don't like our lives, then we must change our perception. Everything else follows.

And this is also where intuition comes into play. When we trust our intuition, we're simply following our soul path. The two are intrinsically linked, and it's impossible for one to be correct while the other is false.

Trust your intuition. Trust your soul path.

13

PERSONAL RESPONSIBILITY

SEVERAL YEARS AGO, a friend of mine raved about Jan, a friend of hers. Jan was a farmer's wife who lived in Missouri. My friend had built a labyrinth and invited many people to her house, and I really looked forward to finally meeting Jan.

When I arrived, Jan avoided me. She wouldn't make eye contact. Toward the end of the evening, she looked at me and said, "It's time you and I had a talk."

We walked outside and Jan said, "Ninety-nine percent of people have choice. You don't. Other people may not know who you are, but I do. I have worked too hard, through too many lifetimes, for you to be in pity-party mode, feeling sorry for yourself, and not doing what you are supposed to do. Open up and let the darkness come after you, instead of after others who can't handle it."

~

Her point? I was in fear mode, preaching only to the groups that wanted to hear me. I had not opened myself up to the groups that didn't want to hear me. I realized that to stay on path, I needed to open myself to everyone, and I did so. Soon everyone began to find me—those who needed me, and those who disbelieved.

What did I learn? Never take anything said personally, good or bad. Every word is simply that, a word with no meaning other than what I give to it.

I've appeared on many national and international radio shows over the last eighteen years. On a few occasions, I received emails afterwards that said, "How dare you charge money for your services," or, "You are a blight on society." I would reply, "Thank you for your opinion, for telling me your feelings."

I learned that if I wasn't making someone upset by what I said, then I probably wasn't fully doing my job. The important thing was to validate their feelings, and not take it personally, nor reply with words that would cause a clog in my body. Remember: any anger or hurt would be stored in my body, not theirs.

To integrate unconditionalism through non-ego and non-judgment into your life, there should be no separation between who you are at work, or anywhere else, and who you are as a person.

I act the same no matter what role I am in—facilitator, woman, mother, or teacher. Americans, especially, subscribe to a theory that they are one way from nine to five, and another way at home.

Resist that thinking. If you are segmented, you are less than a whole person.

I once visited a little boy with cancer in a hospital, where a Reiki master and a therapeutic touch practitioner stood in the room, having worked on the little one all day. I walked in and touched the little boy.

The other two said, "Wait! You didn't protect yourself! You didn't ground yourself."

I looked at them and said, "You are both hypocrites if you are not walking in a loving state every minute of the day."

Think about it: if you need to stop to protect yourself, then you are allowing fear to be a part of your life. If you understand that none of us is solid, then you know that disease is simply a vibration.

Self-protection is a form of shutting down, and it comes from fear. It's a misnomer, because there is nothing to protect yourself from. You cannot take on someone else's problem. Personal responsibility means being responsible for how you conduct all of your life. Be congruent. Open up.

If I am laying of hands on someone for healing, I want that same energy and feeling to go to someone I casually touch in the grocery store. Why should it be any different?

~

Years ago, I received a phone call early in the morning from a father who shared the sad news that his son was dying. Having worked with the young boy for a few months, I had promised him that I would be with him when he passed.

And so I sadly got into my vehicle and drove to the hospital to assist a family as their seven-year-old son was dying of leukemia. I held him in my arms, sang to him, talked to his parents. There was so much love in that room, it was phenomenal.

After he died, his parents and I spent some time in prayer, and talked. The overall question from the parents was, "Why?" Unfortunately, on a human level, there is no "why," there just "is"—an incredibly hard concept for parents who just lost the most precious thing in their life. As we talked and they began to understand that their son hadn't left, he'd simply changed forms, it became easier for them to cope. The grief was still enormous, but their understanding helped take the raw hurt away.

I left the hospital and stopped by the post office on my way home. Inside was an older woman who just looked so sad. When I first spotted her, I realized how lonely and abandoned she felt. No one appreciated her, or took time for her. Maybe she was eccentric, or not too intelligent, but for whatever reason, she did not feel validated as a human being by her friends and family.

Her vibrant blouse matched her eyes, so I walked over to her and told her so. She instantly smiled, thanked me, took my hand, and told me I was her angel. I smiled, and we spoke for a few minutes. That brief conversation—that tiny exchange of energy from me to her—gave her validation of who she was: a beautiful, intelligent soul.

What did it give me? It gave me a smile, a happy essence to know that just a few minutes had changed her perception of life.

Back at home, I took a shower and got ready for a date. My male friend was attentive, showering me with roses, a beautiful dinner, and a truly magical evening of intimacy and a sharing of incredible energies. He gave, I gave, and between the two of us, we created energies of joy, bliss, nurturing, and love.

≋

At the end of that day, it occurred to me that no one had received any different energy from me—not the little boy who passed, not his parents, not the older woman, and not my date. Every single one of them had received identical energy flow from me.

Why? Because none of us knows what will happen to those that we come in contact with. Who gave me the right to unconditionally love one over another? Who told me that I could make a conscious choice as to who deserved more of me than another?

Every single person that I come in contact with in this world deserves all of me—not part of me, but every molecule.

≋

In 2002, I received a phone call from a woman with severe environmental and food allergies. She'd been essentially housebound for over three years, and could only eat five different foods. She desperately needed help.

She and her partner found a "scent–free" bed and breakfast, and traveled to come see me. She reminded my secretary for me to remove any candles, incense, perfumes, etc. I chuckled and told my secretary to reassure Vanessa that everything would be fine.

When Vanessa arrived at my office, I had not altered my usual routine. I had showered with my lavender soap, and the office had its typical incense smell. Nothing was altered because of her fears.

She never said a word about the scents rolling through the office. I made her comfortable in a chair, made her a cup of tea, and we discussed her life as it was currently. What were her desires and goals?

Then we began a Cellular Cleansing. I asked her to imagine walking down some stairs, and she relaxed deeper and deeper. I was actually putting her into a state of light hypnosis.

After two hours of visualization, cleansing up to age five for her cellular memory, she and her partner left my office. They went to a restaurant where cigarette smoke lingered in the air. She ordered pizza and chocolate cake, foods she had not eaten for years.

The next day, we continued our work, finishing up with healing pools. This enabled her to forgive, to receive Unconditional Love for herself, and heal herself with blessed water. All the while, she remained in a light state of hypnosis, using NLP (Neuro-Linguistic Programming) and my energy.

Everyone gets homework, and so I instructed her on what to do for the next thirty days. While she still had to do more visualization when she got home, she was instantly better— eating more foods she never dreamed she'd be able to eat.

She even planned to travel to Brazil via airplane—again, something she'd ruled out for her life.

~

Vanessa made her trip to Brazil six months after her Cellular Cleansing, and is now a guide to the Casa, which means that she brings in people from all over the world to accept healings from John of God. She's also a Certified Associate Practitioner of Patti Conklin, Inc.

Remember: if you seem to be allergic to everything, you're really out of balance. Allergies, whether environmental or food, are learned behaviors. When you have an allergic reaction, your instant thought is, "Oh no, I'm allergic to this." Your body then takes *that* information and continues to make truth of it for the rest of your life, unless your release it with an active vibration.

Most people don't consider what their emotional status was twenty-four hours prior to an allergy event. Their bodies responded to emotions, not smells or specific foods.

It doesn't matter what is out there. For example, my sons understood, growing up, that if one person had the flu, it didn't mean everyone else would catch it.

When I feel flu symptoms coming on, I lie down and say, "Okay, where in my body do I need to work?" I look at how I've been feeling emotionally, and I thank my body for letting me know. I then move the energy through my body, just as you can do with the ColorWorks, and go through the flu in one hour. I again thank my body for making me aware of something I needed to deal with.

Apply the principles of healing to your work, but remember to respect your clients' boundaries, as well as your own. Honor yourself and enforce those boundaries. Give yourself permission to do this work, and get verbal permission to work on someone else.

Seeking Assistance

Some people enlist the help of angels or spirit guides when clearing a blockage. The angel's role is to relay messages and answers from God. The piece of the Creator in all of us has all the information we need. The goal is to trust yourself to listen to that piece. It will tell you everything you need to know.

You're not totally clear to read, even to read yourself. If your body hurts, thank it and ask it what it wants to tell you. If the pain is overwhelming your ability to move energy, ask your body to reduce the pain by fifty percent. If you put energy into a hurting part of your body, and the emotion that comes up is love, peace, serenity, or joy, then you are in denial, or not willing or ready to deal with the issue. Love doesn't create a blockage, ever. It takes about three to four weeks of moving energy every day, or twice a day, to move out an energy blockage.

Most of the seminars I teach are in hotel conference rooms. Sometimes participants ask, "Why don't you do it at a nice, quiet resort or spa, with candles and incense burning and soft mats to sit on?"

Simple: if you can do this work in a hotel, you can do it anywhere, no matter what.

One way I teach people to communicate with their bodies is by using a simple yes/no response system. Spirit, or Father, literally speaks to you through your body.

Sit in a quiet space and ask your body, "Show me yes." Then take a deep breath, and pay attention. Does your toe tingle? Do you have a sweet taste in your mouth? Then, ask your body, "Show me no." Again, what do you sense? A tightening in the chest? A twinge in your head?

You ask your body for a specific response showing yes or no, so you can ask direct questions and receive direct answers. After some practice, like any skill, this will become second nature to you. You may start to say something negative to someone, but feel a pull in your shoulder, or whatever your signal is for no, and choose to honor your intuition and refrain. If you are trying to decide whether reading a book would be helpful to you, a tickle at the base of your neck may signal you to answer it.

By developing the yes/no response system, you start to reconnect with Source. Remember: the soul is here to learn, not give answers. Go to Source with your questions. The reply will come through your body, so pay attention.

14

DUALITY: DARKNESS AND LIGHT

SOMETIMES PEOPLE ASK ME, "If the world operates on the basis of Unconditional Love, then why do bad things happen? Why is there evil?"

Duality must exist. There cannot be light without dark. We appreciate goodness only when we experience evil.

I once got a call from a man on death row who was concerned about his soul after he died. He was imprisoned for the rape and murder of an eight-year-old boy, and I had to visually see and experience the whole event myself as he told me about it. It was very challenging. I spent three hours on the phone with him, and were it not for my experiences with other pedophiles prior to this call, I doubt I would have been able to stay out of judgment with this man.

What he really wanted to know, however, was. "What will happen to my soul when I'm executed?"

I said his soul process would be the same as everyone else—he would cross, he would be in frequency, and he would continue on his soul path to ascension, another reincarnation, or whatever was pre-ordained between the soul and the

Father. His purpose in this life was to create grief and chaos, which he accomplished. Every single person who came in contact with him endured growth because of his actions.

Something that frequently comes up during classes is the subject of reincarnation. The human existence is the most intense and fastest way of learning lessons. On the other side, you can sit and watch, like you might watch a football game, but you learn faster actually playing the game.

With each reincarnation, we get a new set of issues. Some people believe we have karmic issues from previous lifetimes. While we might have stored emotional memories in our subtle energy field from previous lifetimes, we get brand new issues each time around. We each have our own contract with the Creator before we come into this life form.

When someone is really irritating you, and you find yourself angry or in judgment of that person, stop. Take a breath. Do you know that person's contract with God? No? Then may you judge that person?

No, you may not.

The hardest part of change is understanding *what* you need to change.

Generally, men tend to put the vibrational energy of emotional upsets in their brains. They compartmentalize the emotional pain. They don't have to feel the pain, but then they have no connection to the physical signals given by emotion within their bodies. Children take things in differently than adults. For us to take in a betrayal as an adult, it really has to be a huge thing. For a child, it doesn't have to be that traumatic.

If you have asked your body to bring into consciousness what is causing you pain, you must listen, vven if the answer seems silly or ridiculous. Refrain from judging what your body tells you. Can all blockages be released? Absolutely. The only way you can limit yourself is with your brain. Everything is possible, depending upon your perception. If things aren't shifting, if your condition isn't changing, then your body doesn't understand what you're trying to change. You aren't listening, or you haven't learned the lesson yet.

Be creative when moving energy through your body. You cannot do it wrong. It isn't necessary to regurgitate the past, and every gory detail. You should be aware of the emotional memory that you're clearing out, but you don't need to relive it.

When setting goals foryourself, be aware of the words you use. If you're setting your goals as step one, two, three, it often works poorly. It is structural, but also limiting. There's a difference between intent and goals.

Use intent when you're doing something that specifically relates to you, and has nothing to do with anyone else. Realize that when your intent involves another person, you're no longer being an observer, but a controller. You have intuition and intent foryourself. While you can respond to questions from others about their situations, take care not to offer information that was not requested.

15

PRINCIPLES OF HEALING

EARLIER THIS YEAR I had a neighborhood get together with all of my dear friends. One friend brought his brother and sister-in-law, Chris and Lily, who were visiting from New York.

Lily, a pediatric nurse, had suffered from severe diverticulitis for many years. She had missed many days of work, and was anticipating a bowel resection in her near future. She and Chris strongly believed that Western medicine was the only viable option for treating her illness.

We had a wonderful talk about Eastern versus Western medicine.

One day our mutual friend called and said Lily was having a horrible diverticulitis attack, and asked if I could help her. I did, and began pulling the disease from her body. He called Lily to tell her that he had talked to me, and that I had asked him to tell her I was working with her.

Minutes before his phone call, she said, she began to feel like someone was spreading Ben Gay all over her abdomen. Lily told him, "The pain is almost gone."

She returned to her doctor for a checkup soon thereafter. He was surprised to find he could palpate her abdomen without causing her pain. After her last episode of diverticulitis, it had been eight weeks before he could press on her abdomen.

Lily called her brother-in-law. "You're making a believer out of Chris and me," she said. "We are astounded."

A few weeks later, she contacted her brother-in-law again. "I felt a twinge in my abdomen," she said, "so I laid down and talked to Patti about it."

"You called her?" he asked.

"No. I just thought about her and talked to her in my mind."

Lily had popped up in my thoughts that morning. Shortly after she lay down with the twinge in her abdomen, she received an email from me, checking in on her.

~

Diverticulitis is quite often seen in people who keep secrets, preferring not to show all their cards. Seeds and other irritants hide in the pockets of the intestines. Painful inflammation in the bowel is the body's way of telling us that something is hidden.

I worked with this cool entrepreneur here in Atlanta. He had a rare blood disease in addition to Crohn's disease. Six to eight weeks out of every year, he lay in critical condition in the hospital.

When he phoned me for a Cellular Cleansing session, he couldn't keep the skepticism from his voice. However, throughout his lifetime he looked at every Western treatment available, and while he had to lay out much longer than most, given his condition and disease progression, he still wanted to be healed. His physician had heard of me and suggested he contact me for more information. We spoke at length about the process of a Cellular Cleansing, and what it may or may not do for him.

~

He phoned back a few days later. "I'm ready to go forward with a Cellular Cleansing." Having had no background in or experience with alternative modalities, he was just a wee bit skeptical.

After we reached age six in his Cellular Cleanses, he opened his eyes and looked at me, and said, "Patti, is anything really happening? Because this is really easy. All I'm doing is lying here, imagining rooms."

I laughed. "Your body is making tremendous progress."

He stared at me and said, "Oh my God, you're turning green!"

"Yes, your body is dumping tremendous amounts of toxins right now, and we need to stop for today." While he felt wonderful, I was becoming increasingly ill.

When we began the next morning, he looked wonderful, and I felt like I'd been run over by a Mack truck. We proceeded through the rest of the rooms of his life, and then onto the forgiveness pool, the Unconditional Love pool, and the healing pool.

When we were done, he said, "How soon can I get blood work done to verify and validate the cellular process?"

I laughed again. "Wait thirty days."

~

Thirty days later, he phoned to let me know his blood work was 40% increased—much better. He felt wonderful, able to eat nuts and seeds and strawberries and peanut butter, and all the things his Crohn's disease would not allow. Additionally, his blood was much stronger, his platelets looked much better, and his physician was thrilled.

Everything you need to know is inside of you. You were born with all the knowledge you need to live a healthy life and remove disease from your body.

People ask me, "How do I know for sure that it's me telling me information? How do I know I'm not making this up?"

My answer is, "It's you, even if you think you're making it up. Your imagination is part of you."

We're all born with the ability to trust ourselves, and to listen to our bodies, but as we grow, we are taught to doubt ourselves and only trust others. How often were you told, or have you told your children, "Listen to me, I'm the parent?"; or, "Do what the doctor says."; or, "Do what the teacher tells you. She knows best?"

One of the best things you can do for a young child is to say, "What do you think?" Then reaffirm their thoughts. If you continue to tell children what *you* believe, they stop thinking for themselves, and trust others to tell them what to do.

16

THE ACT OF HEALING

As I travel the world, I encourage people to think for theirselves, to let go of what other people think. However, I must say that some in this world are what I would truly categorize as "healers."

I met one while traveling in Brazil. His name is John of God, and he's an incredible man. I watched as he scraped cataracts off a man's eye with a straight razor. I was amazed when he sliced into a woman who clearly had a cancerous tumor in her breast, and then, with no pain whatsoever to the woman, he slammed hemostats up her nose, twisted them 180 degrees, and yanked out the hemostats, along with the tumor from her breast, in the clamp.

What people forget is that with every *gift*, there is a *curse*. For Joao, it was going into convulsions as he would "incorporate"—the Brazilian term for one who joins with a spirit to do healings. Nor does Joao remember, at the end of the day, any of the hundreds of people who stand in line to receive a prescription from him. He has dedicated his life to God and, through the help of the entities (spirits who were once in human form, and are now on an energetic wavelength to assist healers), operated on himself to heal his own stroke. An incredibly courageous man, he has dedicated his life to helping others.

What made Joao real to me were the many people who left Abajianjia without being healed. Just because someone has an astounding gift, doesn't mean that he can heal everyone. The patient's soul plays a critical role in this.

Healing comes from blending both Western and Eastern principles. We are geometry, which is science and math, and vibration, which is spiritual. We bring both aspects into our lives in order to heal, and our bodies truly need both aspects. Eastern is wonderful for pre-disease, and Western is useful for diagnostics.

You need to remember that your hereditary DNA also plays a role in this simple yet complex design we call a body. For example, if you come from a long line of prescription users and meat eaters, your body will respond more to that type of medicine. You may be a vegan, which definitely forces changes in you, but the history of your family genes will remain important.

Your body records every single word and emotion by allowing you a small ache or pain when you first experience a blockage. Have you ever had a heated argument with someone, and when you turned to walk away, felt a pull on your leg, or twinge in your back, or nagging ache somewhere in your body? That's your body letting you know that it has stored an emotional memory.

If we pay attention, and ask our bodies what it needs to tell us, we can clean out the energy blockage so we don't have to deal with it later. What happens more often, after an argument when we're angry or upset, is that we ignore the twinge. Then we often experience pain or disease later, as the body becomes more aggressive in getting our attention, trying to correct the imbalance caused by the blockage.

Our greatest challenge in life is to stay out of judgment with each other and ourselves. When we are in a state of judgment, emotions with low vibrations become trapped in our bodies.

I don't believe in absolutes, but have found some generalizations to be true. To define an absolute is to limit, label and judge. When someone comes to me with a particular ailment, I approach it as though I've never seen anything like it.

People manifest blockages and vibrations differently, but there are a few generalities. For example, in treating more than one hundred thousand clients, I've yet to see someone suffering from an autoimmune disease who didn't have a dominant or suppressive parent.

I had a delightful conversation with a woman who came to see me with crippling arthritis. Although only in her early 30s, she acted as though she was in her 90s. She struggled to straighten out her fingers, to rotate her wrists, to extend her arms, and even to walk. After speaking to her about her life personally, professionally and physically, it was clear she suffered from an autoimmune deficiency disease. Specifically, her immune system had been suppressed.

It took about a year before this patient was able to accept that her mother's love had suppressed her growth. How could her mother's love do such a thing? Her mother never allowed her to do anything by herself. Her mom was so loving that she laid out her daughter's clothes for her every single morning of her school life, from kindergarten until the end of high school. Mom chose what food she should eat, and which hair style she should wear.

This young woman looked at all that her mother did for her as an incredible gesture of love and support. Yet what it really did was take away her ability to choose, to grow, to develop, to express her own thoughts. Yes, her mother truly loved her, to the point of creating a stagnated body which would no longer function without her mother's guidance. Once she accepted it, and utilized her ColorWorks on a daily basis to remove the feelings of suppression, her symptoms abated and disappeared.

Severe rage and hatred are often stored in the spinal area, making it vulnerable to illness and injury. The spine is the pulse of our bodies. Our skeletal structure is supported by the spine. Our nervous system is encased in it, and our bodies' fluid level requirements are all determined from this area.

Hate and rage are the opposite of Unconditional Love. Those who hate and rage are often the most easygoing people in the world . . . until they become angry and lose it. They typically lash out for about two minutes, and then, after the tirade passes, they act as if it never happened, or as if they don't remember it. They literally "put it behind them," and plant the rage in their spines.

Family issues are usually found in the breast, ovaries and uterus for women, and in the prostate and testicles for men. Lower back pain is often caused by a blockage in the kidneys, forcing them to shift and put pressure on the lumbar area of the spine. Some areas of our bodies, such as the liver, do not have nerve endings. In order for our bodies to get our attention, that part of the body sends out tendrils to where we do feel it. For example, a person experiencing nasal congestion may have a lower intestine packed with resentment.

One evening in California, after I had just finished speaking at a Unity church, I was talking with my friend Bob, who hosted an alternative talk show, when his son Jason arrived.

Jason, an accountant, lived in his left-brain and was a linear thinker. He had strong disagreements with his father's beliefs and the content of his show. While he had deep love for his father, Jason thought having a talk show about alternative medicine was a bunch of hogwash.

He had stopped by the church to give his dad a hug, as Jason was scheduled for major surgery in the morning. He had suffered from severe Crohn's disease, an intestinal disorder that causes bleeding, inflammation, and malabsorbtion of minerals and water from the intestine, and was to have a considerable portion of his intestine removed the next day. He had lost twenty pounds in the past three weeks because of the disease, and was in severe pain.

I handed Jason one of my audio books.

He scoffed and said, "I can't go there," and pushed the book back at me, politely and with a smile.

I just smiled back and said, "Who knows, you might decide to listen to it someday."

He chuckled and said, "I doubt it."

"Take it," I said. "Maybe you'll find someone you want to give it to."

He shook his head, laughed and took the book.

The next day, he went in for an MRI before his surgery. His body showed no sign of ever having Crohn's disease. The surgery was canceled.

Sixteen months passed before I heard from Jason. He was still astounded, admitted he had waited so long to contact me because he wanted to see if possibly it was psychosomatic. He stated he had taken one Tums tablet during that time period, but conceded that it was an emotional need at the time, and recognized that he was completely healed.

Happily, he has remained healthy. How did it happen? He listened to the book and began thanking his body for good health. Most importantly, Jason began talking to people about things that upset him, instead of holding it inside, squeezing it down into his intestines. That former path had created the energy of Crohn's inside of his body.

17

DUALITY: EAST MEETS WEST

Embracing the Duality of Eastern and Western Medicine

Whether someone is diagnosed with a disease or just does not feel well, there are many different options for treatment. For example, were Sally to come down with a sore throat, she could go see her family doctor and be tested for a throat infection. She could receive a prescription for antibiotics and painkillers, or go to an acupuncturist for treatment. She could consult a herbalogist, naturopath, or homeopath. She could take natural supplements and herbs to treat her symptoms. She could see a shaman, or visit a Reiki Master or Healing Touch practitioner to balance her chakras. She could take vitamins.

Vibrational medicine using the ColorWorks system can be utilized with any type of treatment program. Only Color-Works, of all the treatments mentioned above, removes the root cause of the sore throat. None of the others address why Sally developed a sore throat in the first place.

A sore throat, as with any illness or discomfort, is the body's way of getting your attention. It is saying, "I need to tell you something. I need you to pay attention."

No matter what healing modality Sally chooses, she can sit quietly and thank her body for bringing this to her attention. Then she can ask her body what it is trying to say, or what she needs to learn from this experience. The body is literal and specific. If she does not get a clear answer, she can ask a different way. She can then remove the core issue from her body using color.

She can still go to her doctor or alternative practitioner for advice, however, and use it. Vibrational healing is not contraindicated in conjunction with any other treatment modality. If she takes a course of antibiotics, she can ask her body what color it needs to boost the effectiveness of the medicine. If she undergoes acupuncture, she can ask her body what color it needs to clear the core issue out of her body while the treatment aligns and balances the energy meridians of her auric field.

As with everything that happens to us, belief is everything when it comes to healing. Each of us chooses our treatment course based on our own individual experiences and belief systems.

During a routine half-hour appointment I had the honor of speaking with a woman in her early 70s. She was soft-spoken and very proper, yet totally delightful. We began by talking about what was going on in her life personally, professionally and physically.

With much joy, she said, "My husband and I have been vegetable farmers, living as vegetarians, my entire adult life. We've raised three beautiful children, and have seven incredibly lovely grandchildren. I've been blessed that the Lord has shown me so much favor in my lifetime."

She moved to her physical ailments, and her voice became quiet, but deep with regret and tears. "When I was twenty-five, I noticed a small lump in my right breast. My doctor said a lumpectomy would be the correct course for me. I was so scared, as it seemed incredibly invasive."

After discussion with her husband, she'd decided to treat this apparent tumor with alternative modalities. She went on a macrobiotic diet, went to an energy worker, took herbs, and went on with her life.

With much sadness, she asked me what I now saw inside of her chest.

I responded quietly, "You know what it is that I see in your chest. It's filled with cancer."

"Yes," she said, "I know, and my doctor confirms it. How much longer do you think I have before the end?"

"Have you had a good and happy life?"

"Yes, I've been so blessed."

"Do you know what will happen as you cross?" I asked.

"Yes, I do, and I'm very much at peace with it."

"Then don't worry how much longer you have," I said. "You've lived a wonderful, calm and fruitful life, one that few get to experience. You didn't make a right choice, and you didn't make a wrong choice—you simply made a choice. All of us will die at some point. You're in your 70s, so hang up this phone, continue your life for however long you have, in peacefulness and joy, knowing that you raised a wonderful family, and that you leave a wonderful legacy behind. And remember: you simply made a choice."

With much love, I wished her well on her next adventure.

~

Did she make the wrong choice? No. Dying is not punishment, it's a part of life, a transition that reconnects us to Source. She held herself responsible for not having the lump removed, but by blaming herself, she sat in judgment of herself. She didn't make a wrong choice, for she made a decision that was right for her in the moment. Life is about choice, not about right or wrong.

Being responsible for your choices does not mean blaming yourself if the outcome is not what you wanted, nor does it mean congratulating yourself for a good outcome. The woman stayed true to her convictions. Yet both Western medicine and alternative therapies can fall into a counterproductive state of mind, one which literally places blame on the patient.

A man and his wife discussed the man's upcoming surgery with their son. The son grew angry and upset, because he felt that surgery was the best course of action for the father he loved dearly.

The man had been diagnosed with bladder cancer, and the doctors said that without surgery, his prognosis was bad. They urgently pushed for a surgical solution, since the cancer hadn't yet metastasized into any other organ. For that reason alone, they felt surgery was the solution. The couple, however, had decided to postpone.

Now, their son felt they had wasted time. They calmly told him that the decision to postpone surgery was their choice, and they were comfortable with it.

"Working with Patti gave us a quality of life," the mother said, "and something to hold on to. It's something we very much believe in." She felt the doctors would have had him buried six months after his diagnosis.

Several years later, the man went ahead with the bladder surgery.

In this case, he took absolute responsibility for his actions, deciding when to incorporate Western medicine into his treatment plan. He lived a full quality of life in the years between his diagnosis and the surgery. His soul lived its Truth, and grew tremendously in that time.

I taught at the University of Missouri in Columbia in 1997, and encountered a judgmental class, comprised of students who were pre-med, Reiki Masters, Pranic Healers, and students who knew nothing about alternative medicine. After the first day of class, I realized I would have to do something drastic to get their attention, as their skepticism hung throughout the room for the entire day.

≈

The second morning, I arrived deliberately late. I held a large McDonalds coffee as I stepped into the auditorium, and the room fell silent.

One brave soul finally voiced what the whole room was thinking. "You know, your energy would be higher if you didn't drink coffee."

As one large nodding head, the class agreed.

"Really?" I asked in a mock surprised voice. "Now, let's see .... What if I were to do this?" I set my coffee down, raised my frequency, and asked everyone in the room to stand up.

They were silent at first, but as they realized they couldn't move, they started panicking, some crying, some yelling, some totally confused.

I smiled at them, pulled the frequency back a little bit, and said, "Stand and take a step forward."

They were able to do so, but only one step. As they all expressed amazement, I asked them if my drinking coffee—beliefs, judgments they'd heard from other people—really affected my ability to control my frequency. Finally, they understood!

One woman in the class later expressed upset at having had breast cancer at twenty-two. After having a double mastectomy six years earlier, her doctors informed her that due to the chemo and radiation, she would no longer menstruate.

The news had devastated her. She'd lost her breasts, and now she would lose her last vestige of womanhood. She'd always wanted children—to "feel" like a woman.

During that day we talked about frequency in class, and discussed beliefs—psychosomatic beliefs—and she approached me at the end of the day.

"Is it really possible to have my body change frequency? Can I get my periods back?"

I gently placed my hands over her ovaries.

She smiled and said she felt a little tingle. Other students were waiting to speak with me, so she left the building.

The third morning of class, we were just beginning when she burst into class. Her frequency was radiant and expanded throughout the entire room.

With tears in her eyes and a tremble in her voice, she screamed, "My period started at 3 a.m. this morning!"

She said she'd immediately phoned her husband, and his response was, "Wait, and this is a good thing?" Then he too, started weeping with joy.

~

One year later, the woman above gave birth to a baby girl, and so it's important to remember that beliefs are just that: beliefs. They can limit, or they can create miracles.

Alternative Medicine

I support all types of Western, Eastern, and alternative therapy modalities, but subscribe to none. I mostly work with medical doctors, and many alternative practitioners are not willing to work with me. Alternative therapies do not have all the answers, but often the purveyors like to think they do. They now sit where physicians were twenty years ago, saying, "We are the only way."

Doctors, however, want to know why something happens as much as I do. Healing comes from blending both Western and Eastern principles—we are all geometry and vibration, and that's it. Geometry is math, and thus scientific. Vibration is spiritual. As with everything we experience as human beings, duality must exist, and we bring both aspects into our life in order to heal.

Alternative therapies can be beneficial to those who subscribe to them and believe they will work. In my work with thousands of clients, I've encountered the full gamut of alternative approaches. It's not important whether I *myself* understand or embrace alternative practices, it's merely important that I work with a patient in the realm of her individual beliefs and values.

Many types of alternative medicine utilize Spirit Guides and Angels. Both help us decipher messages from Source. How can you tell the difference between the two?

Angels have no sense of humor, for they've never walked this Earth in human form. Angels reside in a place of pure Unconditionality—no grief, anger, or sadness, and no laughter or fun. They are serene and straightforward in delivering their messages.

If you're getting messages in the form of a riddle or word play, you're hearing from a Spirit Guide. Although these beings have walked the Earth, they've become Unconditional in the same manner as Angels. Spirit Guides have chosen to interact with and help Souls in human form. They've learned the joy of a good joke or pun while in their human form, and will show a humorous side.

Most alternative therapies such as Crystals, Essential Oils, Flower Essences, Homeopathic, Reiki, or Therapeutic Touch, are passive vibration and deal with the auric energy field outside and around the body. While these therapies certainly make many of their clients feel better, the effects generally do not last. They require multiple visits over time.

Why?

Because the core issue *must* be removed from the subtle energy system in order to remove the cause of the symptoms. Vibration must be used to clear the blocked energy flow. Modalities that balance the chakras alleviate the symptoms, or "fix" the problem in the outer seven layers. They feel wonderful, but do not alter the vibration of the cells, and therefore do not make permanent changes.

For example: often when people get a massage, they start crying or feeling very emotional. That's because the massage is working an emotional memory out of the body and into the auric field. The patient feels relief, but if the vibration is not changed, the emotional memory will settle back into the body after the massage, and soon the symptoms will return.

18

BITS AND PIECES/SOUL FRAGMENTATION

SOME ILLNESSES ARE caused by other types of vibrations stored in the body, including soul fragments, extraterrestrials, unresolved issues from past lives, dark entities and demonic possessions. Two energies cannot occupy the same body, or the energy won't flow.

When we go through especially traumatic events in childhood, a piece of the soul sometimes breaks away and hides in the body. People who have been diagnosed with multiple personalities almost always have one soul that has fragmented, not a committee of souls in one body. Depending on the hormone levels of the person at the moment of fragmentation, the soul fragment could be of the opposite sex.

One woman who attended our conference had suffered a soul fragment when she was two years old, caused by severe emotional abuse. The fragment had remained that age throughout her lifetime. I helped her reintegrate it.

The next morning at breakfast, two women who had been in my class sat glaring at me. I looked questioningly at these ladies, but they ignored me—except for the glaring, of course.

I finally decided to address the situation and approached their table. "Do we have a problem, ladies?" I asked.

"Did you have to put that piece back last night?" one of them said.

"Why, was there a problem?"

"We're her roommates. She kept us up all night, wanting to have a pillow fight, to have a bubble bath, and for us to go outside and climb trees with her. She was a child, all excited and petulant. Now she's up in the room sleeping like a baby, and we feel like we babysat all night!"

I apologized profusely to them and explained why it happened that way. We had a great talk, and when they finally understood what had happened, they were excited for their friend, who had found a piece of her childhood.

Autism is another interesting challenge. Autistic children, in many cases, have a soul which is "tethered" outside of the body—not completely, but partially.

I worked for the first time with a little boy named Brandon, age nine, who had been diagnosed as Autistic when he was four. He couldn't speak, seemed totally unaware of his surroundings, and had no concept of time. He couldn't even perform a little function such as putting his socks on.

That first time I saw him, a thin line came out of his heart center, and his soul floated next to the physical form.

I spoke with his mother, who didn't know much about vibrational work, and gently said, "Your son's soul isn't completely seated into his body. I'm going to gently 'tap' it back in."

As the young boy wandered aimlessly in my office, I followed him and manipulated his vibration, working the soul back into his body. I then asked his mom to bring him back in two months, so I could follow up with him.

On their next visit, the boy walked into my office totally focused.

I smiled and said, "Hi Brandon."

To my astonishment, he responded with, "Hi, Ms. Conklin."

I stopped in my tracks, started laughing, and followed him into my office.

His mom, in a choked voice, said, "In the last two months, he's come to understand words, to speak, to understand the days of the week. This morning, he shocked me and my husband when he came into the bedroom early in the morning. I'd just flown a red-eye in from California, and was exhausted. My husband was in the shower. Brandon had had an accident in bed, and needed to be bathed and put into fresh clothes. He wanted to climb into bed with me, and I asked him to please wait for Daddy to get out of the shower.

"Brandon just left the room. Then, ten minutes later, he walked back in with clean clothes on! For the first time ever, he dressed himself. My husband and I were totally shocked, and started crying. We realized that Brandon was becoming the son we always knew we'd had."

～

One woman in California had fragments like glass shards throughout her body. It was an extraterrestrial, or ET, that had shattered in her body. I had never seen anything like it before this case, and haven't seen one since. It caused her a lot of pain.

I went into her body with bi-location and experienced the pain myself, in order to put the ET back together again so he could go home. It was an incredibly painful experience for me as I felt these glass shards, and it actually took me two hours to complete the process. To this day, I don't understand *how* it happened; I only know that when I completed the process, she was pain free for the first time in ten years.

If there is a specific lesson you need to learn from a fragment, entity, ET, or past life, it's that you can't get rid of them until you learn the lesson. Reintegrating the fragment or removing an entity eliminates the emotional memory and vibration blockage associated with it.

A woman in New Jersey had an intimate lover who broke up with her. She missed him every day, and became sick and called me. I looked at her, and discovered that she had a fragment which was not hers held in her kidney. It was her ex-lover's energy, so I questioned her a great deal about their relationship.

She said it was tumultuous and abusive, but she felt strongly that in their past lives together, she'd been mean to him and that, in this lifetime, it was her turn to suffer. She wasn't sure about having the fragment removed, but after a few minutes of discussion, she agreed.

I removed the fragment and handed it to an angel standing next to her, but the angel just stood there instead of taking it back to the man. I asked the angel why it hadn't moved, but got no response.

Two days later, the woman called hysterical. "I'm happy! I'm supposed to be miserable. I need it back! I'm supposed to feel the pain. I know it. It's my turn to suffer. You *must* put it back!" Apparently, she hadn't learned what she needed to yet, and felt the need for continued ill health, to be punished.

The angel was still standing there holding the fragment, so I pushed it back in. It was difficult, requiring a lot of energy.

Several months later, she called again. "I'm dying," she said. "I need you to take it out."

"No," I said. "Do it yourself. I showed you how, once."

She must have figured it out, because the last I heard, she was still alive.

This brings up another thought to keep in mind, and it's one we've touched on over and over in these pages: watch your verbiage. Your body makes literal truth out of everything you say.

People in a romantic relationship often say, "You will always be with me," or, "You will always have a piece of my heart." The man's soul fragment found its way into the woman's kidney because of something he said to offer it to her. Maybe he said, "You'll always be a part of me," or, "A part of me will always be with you."

People who receive organ donations also receive some of the donor's energy, and occasionally a fragment of the donor's soul.

I worked with a ten-year-old girl who received a heart transplant from a thirteen-year-old girl who had been murdered, and subsequently began having terrifying nightmares. Nothing seemed to stem the detailed nightmares. The police working on the donor's murder case had a suspect, but no murder weapon, and they were having trouble putting together a strong enough case for a an arrest.

The little girl's mother called me for help, and I asked her to take her daughter to the police station. The girl vividly recounted her nightmares, describing in exact detail what had taken place when the victim was murdered, and where the murderer had hidden the knife. The memory of the incident had been stored in the murdered girl's heart. Once we removed the fragment, her nightmares stopped.

Those who've had organ transplants must remove the energy of the donors. We reject organs because they have the donors' subtle energy field, and two energy fields cannot exist in one body.

If you've had an organ transplant, ask your body what color it needs to remove the donor's subtle energy field. Work with that, and then ask what color you need to place your own subtle energy field within the new organ. Your body will then have a much smaller chance of rejection, as you'll have integrated your energy field into new flesh in your body.

People often ask me about blood transfusions. Generally, blood carries little vibrational memory. The act of giving blood is rarely perceived as traumatic to a volunteer donor, and soul fragmentation is uncommon.

19

TRAUMATIC FRAGMENTATION

A TWENTY-THREE-YEAR-OLD woman from New Jersey had been diagnosed with multiple personality disorder many years before. She displayed seven distinct identities, and had worked with a doctor and psychologist for several years, with little improvement.

One afternoon, the doctor and psychologist were working with her at home, attempting to integrate the personalities, but weren't having much success. They gave me a call.

"When she was growing up," the psychologist said, "her father locked her in a closet—from age four to twelve. He was a sheriff's deputy, and only let her out to rape her. She ate, slept and defecated in the closet. She's been through extensive psychotherapy for many years, but with little improvement, I'm afraid."

I asked to speak with the woman over the phone. We spoke for a while, and then a gruff, aggressive male personality emerged, abrasive and hostile. Her voice lowered, and her speech was thick with obscenities.

The personality said, "I'm Sam. Just what do you think you're doing?" He sounded like an old 17th century woodcutter.

I said, "Your presence in the woman's body is keeping her from having a happy, functional life."

Sam was a fragment of another soul who had lived over two hundred years ago. When the woman's soul left her body as an act of self-preservation, Sam had come right in.

"I'm the one who took over during his abuse," he said.

"He's no longer here," I said. "She doesn't need your protection anymore."

He smirked. "I'm the only one that saved her."

"But now you're killing her. May I have your permission to put you back where you belong?"

"If you think you can do it," Sam said, taunting me.

I asked him several more times for permission, and finally, he agreed. I asked him to put the doctor and psychologist on the phone.

"You guys need to leave the room," I said.

"We want to see it," they said, and set the telephone down.

I opened my heart center and began moving a tremendous amount of energy to remove Sam's fragment from the woman's body. After a few moments, I heard the doctor and psychologist yelling in the background. "Stop! Let us out! We're against the wall!"

I stopped to let them leave the room, then immediately went back to work.

After several minutes, Sam was gone and the other six fragments of her own soul were integrated into one.

The woman cried. "It's so quiet," she said. "How am I going to live without the noise, and all the talking?"

"Now you'll need therapy more than ever," I said. "You have to create a new life and learn about silence."

≈

Multiple personalities are almost always caused by fragments of the same soul, not a committee of souls in one body. Sam was a past life fragment, and the other six fragments were from her soul in this lifetime.

The woman continued her therapy with the psychologist, and today, she is a completely healthy wife and mother of two.

When people sustain a particularly intense trauma, especially in childhood, one or more pieces can break off from the soul and lodge in the body. Because everything we experience is based on perception, it doesn't even have to be a particularly horrific event. If a child perceives an event as overwhelming, the soul may be affected.

The piece of soul that breaks off does not mature. The fragment may be male or female, depending on the levels of hormones in the body at the time of the event; all of us have testosterone and estrogen in our bodies. A growing boy, for example, may experience a surge of estrogen when a soul fragment is formed, making the fragment seem feminine or female.

Not all soul fragments manifest as dramatically as multiple personalities. However, a soul fragment should be addressed and removed from the body if it is discovered. Fragments stop growing at the moment they splinter off. Their vibration does not match the ever-changing energetic vibration of your subtle energy system, and they create a blockage. The second law of physics states that no two pieces of matter can occupy the same space at the same time. This is as true in the subtle energy system as it is in the material world.

I was teaching a conference with my dear friend Dick Sutphen when I did a group healing with a volunteer. She had experienced a soul fragment when she was five years old, but didn't have any symptoms of multiple personality disorder. Since the fragment had splintered off at age five, she really had never experienced play in her life. The fragment, the part of her soul that was necessary to learn how to play, wasn't there.

I asked if she ever felt like there was a "piece" missing in her life, and she affirmed that, indeed, she'd never understood how people could play. I reintegrated the five-year-old fragment, which was hiding in her left breast, back into her soul.

Her eyes began to sparkle, she smiled, and truly, her face changed and became younger. People attending the conference were stunned as they watched her for the rest of the weekend, reclaiming her life.

If there is a specific lesson your soul needs to learn from having a soul fragment, or someone else's soul fragment, you cannot reintegrate or remove the piece until you learn the lesson. Also, rejoining a soul fragment to its source will remove the emotional memory and vibration blockage from your body.

Schizophrenia

Schizophrenic people often see the world just as I do—patterns of vibration and energy. Schizophrenics talk to beings most of us cannot see. They cannot distinguish between worlds, between souls in human and other form. Many people with schizophrenia have my sight, but not the ability to comprehend what they see, and it scares them.

A woman called me and made an appointment for her paranoid schizophrenic son. My secretary had left early that afternoon, and he was my last appointment.

In walked a six-foot-eight, three-hundred-pound man. His mother had told me that he was taking his medication, but I looked into his body and saw no traces of medication anywhere.

We had a nice conversation in my office, until his eyes began to glaze over. I tried to get him to reconnect with reality by creating a small amount of motion. He reached over and grabbed my right breast. He twisted it hard, as though he would twist it off of my body. My energy surged, but I stayed in control. If I had let my energy surge toward him, I could have seriously hurt or killed him.

The pain was excruciating, but I kept speaking to him in soft, reassuring tones while containing my energy, all the while aware of severe lymph tissue damage in my own body. Although it seemed like forever, he finally let go about three minutes later.

His mother, who had dropped him off at my office and gone to lunch, hadn't bothered to tell my secretary during the initial phone call that he becomes sexually violent when he goes into a paranoid state.

I had two more sessions with the man—over the phone. It was clear he was operating from a past life memory. Once he released that karma of his schizophrenia, he went on to have a normal, healthy life. Today, he is a police officer in Maryland.

Addiction

While most forms of illness and disease can be healed, an addict is almost never cured. An addictive personality will always be an addictive personality. Addicts show a tremendous amount of co-dependency, and are trying to fill a void within themselves. These people can be redirected to more productive addictions, such as cleaning the house or pursuing a hobby or career, but they are no less addicts than when they were using alcohol, drugs, food, or sex.

Of all addictions, sex addiction is the most difficult to resolve. Sex is everywhere, part of a normal intimate relationship. Someone can live a full life without alcohol or drugs by choosing to never touch those items again. However, most relationships can't survive without sex.

Sex addicts, therefore, if they are an active part of society, more often than not find it difficult—or almost impossible—to balance their participation. This makes sex addiction the most challenging and truly pervasive in our culture, for an addict must always have something to take the place of whatever was removed.

Behavioral Disorders

Obsessive-Compulsive Disorder can almost always be cured. It's usually an irrational fear expressed as fixation on one particular behavior, such as collecting items or washing one's hands repeatedly. The irrational fear can be removed from an individual's cellular structure.

Many mental disorders mirror each other, differing in only one particular aspect. For example, borderline personality disorder and bi-polar disease both foster elements of co-dependency, and each manifests significant and sudden changes in mood and behavior from one moment to the next. The difference is that individuals with borderline personality disorder retain no recollection of the things they said or did during an especially manic or depressive state.

In terms of chemical imbalance, borderline personality usually results from childhood trauma or abuse. Multiple personality disorder occurs when more severe abuse or trauma occurred in childhood. Bi-polar disorder and depression are usually hereditary, but certainly can also be caused by trauma or abuse.

20

FAITH AND BELIEF

MANY PROPHETS PROCLAIM THEIR visions of humanity on a grand scale. They predict Armageddon, Jihad, or the beginning of Revelations. We get so caught up with other people and other countries that we forget that change begins within ourselves. Healing can only take place within our own bodies.

In order for big changes to occur, a little change must happen every day on a personal level. People must get back to the basics of how they interact with themselves. It's wonderful to give a donation to feed hungry children in a faraway country, but did you hug your own child today? How did you interact with the bagger at the grocery store this morning? Did you tell your spouse or lover that you appreciate them? Did you let your co-worker know that you're aware of their contributions?

When I get off a plane, I don't care how turbulent the flight was or how bumpy the landing, I always say to the pilot, "Thank you so much for getting us here safely." Before I board a long flight, I buy sweets for the flight attendants, and give them my favorite chocolate-covered blueberries.

People appreciate kindness so much, but while many of us think nice thoughts, we rarely exhibit kindness to those we're thinking about.

When you pull up to that takeout window, do you sincerely tell the cashier that you hope they have an incredible day, or do you just assume they're in a hurry, or unworthy of your effort at kindness. Or do you simply not even think about that person as a mother, father, child, brother, or sister?

Miracles are poised to happen all around us, every day. When people open themselves to the occurrence of miracles, they happen. They're always here. Most of us don't have a strong enough belief system to see them, or to have them manifest. We must understand that they're everywhere, not just in special places. Everywhere.

Dreams and visions happen to all of us. If my history is faulty, I cannot see the dream for what it is. For example, say I have a fear of snakes, and one night I dream of snakes. I can only interpret the dream in terms of my history with snakes, and my fear of them. Snakes may signal change in a positive and exciting way, but because I fear them, I miss the real meaning of the dream, and feel fear instead.

People often ask my religious denomination. I embrace them all and subscribe to none. It doesn't matter what I believe; it only matters what you believe.

Every master—every single one—has always taken the people back to God, and it didn't matter if that was Buddha, Jesus, Shiva, or Abraham. Metaphysical types cringe when I talk about Jesus, because some types of religious fanaticism have given Christianity a bad name. I adore Buddha, and believe that on some levels he was more profound than Jesus. While I'm a Christian, I closely identify with the lifestyle ideas of Zen Buddhism, so in reality, I consider myself a Christian/Buddhist.

≈

Nancie is an extraordinary woman, an atheist raised in an atheist family, a practicing hypnotherapist who speaks at many conventions around the country.

At age six, she was diagnosed with a rare form of Muscular Dystrophy. The MD created challenges for her throughout her life, and by age thirty-five, she was confined to a wheelchair.

I'd always seen Nancie whipping throughout the hotels on her scooter, a delightful woman who never allowed her disability to get the best of her. For years, we spoke about our kids and our profession, but never once touched upon her MD. I always figured that when someone is ready to work with me, they'll bring it up; it's not my place to offer help.

In 2003 she came up to me and said it was time for her to work with me. I just smiled and told her to give my secretary a call, and she traveled to Atlanta a short time later, staying in a handicapped-equipped room.

I usually asked my clients to decide "who" they would like to assist them—angels, guides, etc., but as an atheist, she didn't hold such beliefs. We went with leprechauns and helpers, and that first evening, we worked through to her age four.

When I arrived at her hotel room in the morning, she greeted me at the door—no cane, no wheelchair, no scooter! With an impish edge to her voice, she asked, "Would you like a soda?"

"Yes," I said.

She walked past me, out the door, down the hallway, and returned a minute later with a soda. I was stunned.

We finished up her remaining years that day, ending up in the healing pool, which would be her homework for the next thirty or so days.

She left Atlanta and flew back to Virginia, and within ten days, put her wheelchair and scooter equipment in storage. She increased her muscle mass within the next month by 33%, her eyesight improved, and she developed arches in her feet. Her doctors were stunned.

Two years later, she danced at her daughter's wedding, and she now participates in ballroom dance competitions, fully functioning and 45 pounds lighter—a completely new woman.

≈

Again, it doesn't matter what you believe, as long as you believe in *something*. Is there a Creator, or are we all just in the here and now, with no afterlife? It doesn't matter. What does matter is how you feel about your own ability to know.

Any Religion

I received an interesting phone call one day from Serbia. I spoke to a gentleman who was a chiropractor, and he was having a challenge with his 90-year-old mother. She was still active but, despite his best efforts, continued to suffer back pain.

He said, "Patti, it's really important for you to work within my mother's belief systems. I think she'll listen to you, as long as you incorporate what you're saying with her faith."

I laughed. "As long as you tell me what your mother's belief systems are, then I have no problem working with that."

"My mother is an Orthodox Serbian Jew."

I had no idea what that meant, so we spent a few minutes talking about what an Orthodox Serbian Jew believes.

Then his mother got on the phone. What an incredibly precious woman. Her soul just lit up. Even with thousands of miles between us, I could see her face so clearly in front of me—such a beautiful woman; I couldn't help but smile.

In halting English, she spoke of how much her back pained her.

I explained to her ColorWorks, and that I was going to move energy into her body at the same time that she visualized color. I truly believed that we understood each other, and I gently started moving energy into her body as she moved color, and I visualized the color from her home in Serbia.

After approximately five minutes of this work together, I asked her to set the phone down and walk around, allowing her body to readjust, and then to come back and let me know how she was feeling physically and emotionally.

After eight minutes or so of silence, I said, "Hello? Hello?"

Her son's voice came over the line, and he was chuckling softly.

I said, "Where is your mom? I asked her to come back to the phone after she'd walked around for a few minutes."

He just continued laughing, and finally said, "She's on her hands and knees, washing the kitchen floor, because that's when her back really hurts her, when she washes the floor."

I could hear his muted voice as he gently asked his mother how her back was feeling as she so diligently scrubbed the floor.

Her response was, "Good, good, no hurt."

It didn't matter that she was an Orthodox Serbian Jew. It didn't matter that I was a Christian/Buddhist. We were able to find a middle ground, a mutual respect, and accomplished our task.

So many beautiful people walk this Earth that I'll never have the chance to meet in person, yet I feel blessed that I've been allowed to see as much as I have throughout my life.

We get caught up in whatever religion we subscribe to, rather than how we actually interact every day in our lives. None of the masters would have wanted us to stop at religion. Every single one of them promoted living every day in a state of unconditionality.

People want something to believe in. Many go to church every Sunday, or spend an hour or two meditating each day. At church, they are told that all will be forgiven, yet these same people go out into the world and spend the rest of their week living in judgment of others. They expect to receive forgiveness during church for their behavior while they were not at church. The problem with that is two-fold: first, life is perfect, so there is nothing to forgive; second, being good for two hours doesn't give someone permission to stay in a state of ego and judgment the rest of the time.

I know many people who say they were apostles or Mary Magdalene in a past life. People want to feel special, and if they don't stand out in this lifetime, they can safely assume they stood out in another lifetime. People often blame their karma, or past lives, to justify their behavior. They are disappointed with their lives, and think it would be better if something were different.

I used to stand on the street corner and watch people's thoughts go into their bodies. "If only I had more money," and, "If only I had more education," and a constant string of "if only." If only some*one* had fulfilled some*thing*. They have a hard time taking responsibility.

The bottom line is that each individual makes their own choice. Who can we look at to assign responsibility? I can only look at me. It's hard to be at peace with everything the way it is; we always want something different.

The whole path of spiritualism is how you can be at peace, no matter what is taking place around you. Meditating or going to church every week is fine, but not enough. Be at peace with where you are.

None of us can ever see the whole, great picture. That's okay. We don't have to know *why* things are; we just have to trust that they are. God, no matter the origin or definition, asks us to find that deep peace within ourselves, to understand that everything is perfect no matter what happens. We can maintain a deep knowing peace on the inside, even when our external world is falling apart.

Karma

I recall one of my dearest friends as she faced her last days in physical form. Sonia worked as an events planner for a small company. She was dedicated to her work and loved by many, many people.

Sonia's company planned a tour of Egypt, and she felt a strong desire to go on the trip. They tried to dissuade her, as she was needed for other things, but she felt such urgency about it that the company relented.

She and the other members of the tour group had a complete physical before embarking. I happened to be visiting her right before she left, so I looked at her body, and she was perfectly healthy.

She was in Egypt for ten days, during which time she developed a tumor in her left breast the size of a baseball.

Upon returning, she immediately had surgery to remove the tumor and the breast, and started chemotherapy. Yet this rare, aggressive form of cancer wouldn't quit. Within a month, she had developed an even larger tumor in her right breast.

We were all totally devastated as her body essentially dissolved before our very eyes. She wasn't in pain, but she could feel her life force slipping away. She knew she was dying, and that there was no way to stop the process.

She phoned me one night. "Patti, my body is disintegrating. I can't keep going anymore. What happened to me?" The ensuing silence on the phone line was dense.

I said, "Sonia, when you entered the Queens chamber, I saw something—almost like a virus—vibrating in the southeast corner of the room. As I watched, it floated over to you and entered into your lungs, as if it had been waiting for you for thousands of years."

She spoke so softly I struggled to hear her next words. "Patti, I never told anyone that. When I was in the Queens chamber, I did feel something come into my lungs. I thought it was my imagination."

~

There is no doubt that Sonia experienced a direct Karmic response to something that had occurred millennia ago. Her Karma was fulfilled, and she passed with dignity, as gracefully as she had lived.

21

THE DAY GOD'S TRAIN STOPPED

SEVERAL YEARS AGO, I had a profound dream. I rode on a train with three couples. Each man looked exactly like the others, and each of the women looked alike. Each couple was traveling with a son, and each son looked the same. Everyone had different personalities, but it appeared as though one couple with a son had been produced in triplicate.

The train traveled slowly, and many paranormal activities took place onboard, such as a face coming out of a book. The passengers wanted to stop and get help, but I said we'd be all right if we stayed on the train.

A white stallion ran next to the train, and one of the men climbed out the window and jumped onto the horse's back in an effort to go get help. As soon as he landed, the horse began screaming and sank into a bog. They both sank away, out of sight.

The train stopped, and everyone suddenly vanished, but Jesus and Mother Mary appeared. Throughout my life, Jesus had appeared to me in a dream during the most pivotal changes in my life, but this was the first and only time they appeared together.

Jesus said in a near-whisper, "This train is off the track."

I looked out the window and down at the track, and could see that it was off the track by an inch or two.

"I now give you a choice," Jesus said. "You may get off this train and live your life as a normal human. Or, if we put this train back on the track, you will dedicate and devote the rest of your life to the work. You may ultimately lose your soul as a result of this work."

While I didn't hesitate, I did get chills when I answered. "Go ahead and put the train on the tracks."

I'd always felt like my life was God's, and had known since I was seven that there would come a time when I would do whatever He asked of me.

≈

That was over eighteen years ago, and so much has happened since then. I've dedicated my life to helping others. Sometimes they appreciate it, sometimes they don't think I did enough, and sometimes they don't believe anything happened. Through all of that time, I've held to my faith and belief that *everything* is as it should be. *I know* changes happened; it just comes down to this: did it happen the way the client expected it to happen, or did it happen exactly the way God meant?

How do you really know your life path? How do you really know the purpose of your existence? You don't, and that's sometimes the challenging part of life: to live, even though you have no clue as to what you're doing!

Guidance

Recently I was at a friend's party, where someone asked me, "How do you know when you're guided in your life?"

"When I'm coming into a transitional point," I said. "This is the hard part: having the patience to sit back and wait. Jesus comes to me, even though it's rare. I know it will be Him who delivers the information, so I sit back and wait."

Jesus normally comes to me in dreams, and God appears when I am awake. Jesus has appeared to me infrequently over the years, only on rare occasions, when I was awake.

I had been sleeping about an hour every two nights over an 8-week period. I'd been waiting for Jesus to visit me in a dream, but I hadn't been able to sleep.

When I arrived home from that party, the light on my answering machine was blinking. Almost no one knew my unlisted home number; my friends called me on my cell phone.

I scrolled the caller ID, which said, "God's Son." God's Son had called more than once. *Oh how wondrous!* The number was, obviously, unlisted and a nonfunctioning number. I showed it to my secretary and my friend Richard Sutphen, who was visiting. I phoned my friends at the party, and they were all stunned and disbelieving, until they came over to see it during the next few days.

Jesus had let me know that he was nearby. What a wonderful way to be shown that I was not alone. I will never forget that night for as long as I live.

Eight years ago, I spent one of the most exhausting two days of my life in Santa Barbara, California. A man had phoned my office requesting an appointment. Typically, I no longer saw people in person while on the road, other than to do a Cellular Cleansing. However, as I was telling my secretary to tell him no, Father spoke quietly to me, and said that I would see this man.

≈

After I arrived in Santa Barbara, this man came to my hotel room and we sat out on the balcony. I could clearly see his agitation and fear, and an emotional sickness in his eyes that made my stomach clench.

I said, "How can I help you?"

He fidgeted, tapped his foot on the floor, and bit his lip. "You see, ma'am, I have a position as an official in a nearby town. There's a warrant currently out for my arrest, for indecent exposure."

As I looked at this man, anger began to stir deep within my soul, and an intense dislike began to form in my stomach. I attempted to clear my thoughts as he continued talking.

"You see, I like to date people who are younger than me, and—"

"Why is there a warrant out for your arrest?"

He stared for a moment, and said, "I've been having intimate relations with under-aged children who live on the streets." Before I could respond, he said, "These children are living on their own, independent of parental influences, and so therefore able to make choices on their own." As if that justified his acts. He felt he was the victim in this situation, and not the perpetrator.

I collected my thoughts, then spoke quietly, ignoring my own anger and upset. I attempted to explain that anyone under the age of eighteen was considered a child, and that what he was doing was actually statutory rape.

He shook his head rapidly. "Oh no, oh no, that's not the case. These individuals are no longer under the guidance of a parent, and so therefore are making their own choices in life. The same rules don't apply."

I looked at him with absolute disgust. We'd been speaking together for about thirty-five minutes, and he still didn't understand that what he was doing was wrong.

"Why were you so insistent upon seeing me?"

"I heard you on a radio show," he said, "and I knew you were the one person who would not judge me, and that you could possibly help me make the authorities understand."

I finally just bowed my head, for there was no way I could make him understand, and prayed. "Father, I am so sorry. Apparently, I am not as advanced as I thought I was."

I reached over and touched the man's arm, and he flew back six feet and hit his head on the wall. I'd done it on purpose, and it was the first—and only—time I'd ever used my gift to hurt someone.

I kept my voice low, my tone even. "You have a choice right now: turn yourself in, or I am going to rip you to shreds."

The man scrambled for the phone, blood oozing from the cut on the back of his head, and called the police.

⁓

I felt a deep and terrible despair after that incident. I'd had energy bursts escape when I was shocked or scared, but never had I been so consumed with anger. I so despised him that I *knew* he would be hurt when I touched him.

I wasn't proud of my behavior, and spent two days in a fetal position, questioning my ability to be a servant of God's purpose.

A few days later, I boarded an airplane for the flight back home to Georgia, still in a state of utter despair. I looked out the window, crying softly, and asked myself how I could do this work if I'm so angry.

I looked up and Jesus was standing there, holding a white rose. He leaned over and kissed my forehead. "Thank you, Sister, I know you are exhausted." He laid the rose on my lap. The rose was real.

The man next to me began crying. We were the only two who had boarded the airplane. "Was that Jesus?"

"Yes," I said. We both looked at the rose, still in my lap. It was an emotional moment. The rest of the passengers boarded, and I wept quietly, overwhelmed with love and security.

As the plane took off, the gentleman reached out to me as asked, "Would you allow me the honor of holding you?"

He wrapped his arms around me, and I stayed there for three hours, crying softly into his shoulder.

After we landed in Atlanta, I walked to the next gate for the last flight. While waiting, I kept myself separate from the rest of the passengers. I was emotional and mentally exhausted, wondering how I would get the strength to get in my car and drive home from the airport.

It would be a short, twenty-eight minute flight, but it was already 1 a.m. as I climbed the stairs of the plane with the white rose in my hand. I looked toward my seat in the back of the plane, 7D, and at the man sitting in 7C.

Father was already speaking to me about working with this man.

I was feeling totally split emotionally. Part of me stood there thinking, *I cannot do anymore work. I'm just too exhausted and emotionally spent. I feel resentful, bitchy, and furious.* The other part of me was totally serene, calm, fully aware, and engaged at this next incredible task laid out before me.

After all, Father had once said, "You will always have enough energy to do what you need to do."

⁓

I sat down next to the man in 7C. The book he was reading was open to a page that read across the top: Life is a wondrous adventure.

I reached over and underlined the sentence with my finger. "Isn't it?"

"I guess," he said.

I underlined it again: Life is a wondrous adventure. "Isn't it?"

"If you say so," he mumbled.

Again, I put my finger under the sentence. "Why isn't it?"

"I was watching you while we waited at the gate," he said. "I'm a mechanical engineer, and love to observe people. I've come to the conclusion that you're not like other people."

I smiled and ran my finger along the page of the book again, and quietly asked, "Life is a wondrous adventure, right?"

"Let me tell you about my life," he said. "I was in Vietnam. My three best friends were blown up in front of me. It took me two days to get their blood and guts off my body. Every single night since that day, I've had the same nightmare, reliving that horrible event."

"What is your belief system?" I asked.

"I grew up Catholic, and my wife is Baptist. I don't believe in Jesus. I can't believe there's anything that's good."

"Have you been diagnosed with post-traumatic stress disorder?"

The man nodded.

"If you would like, I could take some of that from you. Would you allow me to?"

He a paused for a moment, and then nodded his agreement.

I put my hand onto his left shoulder and started pulling the memories from his cells.

"This is weird," he said. "I can feel a vacuum sucking from my toes up through the inside of my body."

I pulled energy from his body for a minute or two. "Life is a wondrous adventure," I said again, and smiled.

"If I wake up in the morning, I'm successful. If I die, I'm unsuccessful."

"So you're telling me that if I get killed in a car accident on my drive home tonight, then my life was unsuccessful?"

He paused. "I may have to rethink this."

The airplane landed, and as I got up to leave, I handed him my business card, along with the white rose, and disembarked from the airplane.

Feeling totally numb by now, I drove the hour home.

≈

In the morning, my office phone rang at eight. Normally, I avoided picking up the office phone, but not this morning.

I heard a soft, gentle crying. "So what happened?" I asked.

"I got to my hotel room and lay down," the man from the small plane said. "I started thinking about my friends, and started the usual dream, where they're blown up right in front of me. Then, I was no longer dreaming. I was awake. I sat up in bed and turned on the light. Jesus was standing there.

"He didn't say anything to me. He just walked around the side of the bed and sat down on the edge. I felt the bed give under the weight of him. Without speaking, He laid his hand over the same area you did, and I felt a much stronger suction. After a few minutes, the suction stopped, and he said, 'Now go and live your life in joy.' Then he was gone.

"I wanted to share that with you. I cried for hours, and then exhausted, fell asleep. As I began to dream, for the very first time, I dreamt of my wife and son."

~

We spoke for little while longer, and he truly helped me to understand that, no matter how exhausted I might be feeling, there would always be enough energy to be the conduit for a miracle.

Your faith and belief are vital to who you are as a human being. I'm not talking about a *specific* religious canon; I'm talking about what you know as a human being. You may be an atheist with a strong belief that there's nothing after you get placed in the ground. And that's truly wonderful; it's okay. What's important is that you know what you believe.

People tend to think of faith and belief as religious modalities, and I'd really like to separate those out. They're not at all religious items. Faith and belief has to do with what you call upon, when you dig down deep within yourself, which allows you to make a stand on any challenging item in your life.

If you turn in prayer and meditation to a Master who has walked this earth, great! If you turn to a dear friend, or an advisor whom you deeply trust, then this too is great. Just trust that *you* know exactly what needs to happen. Attempt to turn *within* yourself . . . for you truly have all the answers.

I will end this chapter with one of the most incredible experiences I've ever had. Even as I write this today, I can still feel the imprint on my hand.

≈

First thing one morning, a nun walked into my office with Stiles disease, a rare auto-immune disease similar to lupus.

After a few minutes of discussion, I heard Father say to me, "Take this disease from her."

I had a full schedule that day, and taking the disease from her body would wipe me out for the rest of the day. The other clients who were scheduled needed me, and I wouldn't have the strength to do it all. So I did something I rarely do.

I asked her, "Could you come back at four o'clock?" With a little bit of embarrassment, I added, "God told me to take this from you, but I can't take it right now, as I have two cancer patients coming in today who will need a tremendous amount of concentration from me."

The nun had never dealt with alternative/vibrational medicine before. Her doctor had recommended that she come see me, and she trusted him, but as I explained the situation, she looked puzzled and reluctant. Still, she agreed to come back later that day.

She returned at four that afternoon, and I apologized again. She graciously accepted my reasoning as I explained to her that I had been given direct instructions regarding what to do with her.

I laid my hand on her solar plexus, and began pulling the disease from her body. As I do something like this, and given the specific instructions from Father, a hole opens up in the palm of my hand, and I feel as though a vacuum is sucking out the disease.

I felt sicker by the moment, with the disease coming into my body, and doubted whether or not I would have the strength to pull it all from her body.

Suddenly, Mother Mary appeared right next to me. I was stunned and blessed all in the same moment. She placed her hand over my right hand. I could feel it! It was no different than another person walking in the room and laying their hand on mine, warm and solid—a miracle.

The nun saw and felt her also, and softly sobbed. Both of us sat in awe at Mother Mary—such a serene, loving, accepting, healing presence. With her hand over mine, we pulled the disease from the nun with little effort. As the disease flowed into me, Mother Mary continued to smile gently, and the nun continued sobbing softly as she looked at the most inspirational being she had ever seen.

After our session, and after we both had time to digest the miracle that had just taken place, I explained to the nun that I was stunned, as Mother Mary had never been a Deity who would come and assist me.

The nun explained that Mother Mary was important to her, and was who she prayed to every single night.

≈

It was the only time Mother Mary materialized for me while working on a client.

I stayed in touch with that nun, and years later, she remained free of Stiles. It had happened from the moment she walked into the office.

I'll forever be grateful for such a wondrous experience.

22

THE OTHER SIDE

A BIG QUESTION ON almost everyone's mind is what happens when we die. Is there a heaven? A hell? Through the years, I've observed over two hundred individuals as they transitioned from this life form to the Other Side. My sight has allowed me to watch the soul literally leave the body and make that transition.

Contrary to popular opinion, the Other Side is not a place we go to when we die. The Other Side coincides with our every breath. It co-exists with our reality. It's part of our world that we do not see.

Everything is vibration and geometry, including the Other Side. What you see when you die is what you *believe* you will see. If a Christian believes Jesus is coming for him, he will see Jesus. A person can see relatives, deities, Moses, Abraham, Buddha, or even nothing at all.

It's like a fog bank. When you look into the whiteness of the fog, eventually you might see a shape. The more you see it, the clearer it becomes. The image you see is real. Someone might look into the same fog bank and see a different shape. Fog is still fog. The vibration of the other side is still just that—vibration and geometry.

Is there an actual Heaven where we go when we die? No. First of all, we don't actually go anywhere. We simply transition from one energy form to another. Second, someone who believes in Heaven will see the vibration of the Other Side, and it will appear as Heaven to that person. If, in his mind, angels have wings, he will see angels with wings. If another individual imagines angels without wings, then wingless angels will greet him.

A young man named Eric, who was dying of AIDS-related congestive heart failure, called and asked for my help. He'd heard me on a radio show more than six years prior to this event, and had kept my name with him throughout those years.

He came from a conservative, born-again Christian family, but he was a staunch Satanist. He said he wanted to talk to someone who could love him for who he was, and not judge him for his beliefs, and for that person to be with him when he passed.

I laughed and told him I considered myself a Christian/ Buddhist, but that I could handle his request. We both chuckled on the phone.

He was an incredibly nice guy, and we spent many hours talking about life, life after death, where a soul goes, and what it all means. He was intelligent, loving and caring, but his family remained stagnant and unyielding. As born again Christians, they felt strongly in their beliefs.

I watched the struggles between the father and son during this time period, and I began to see a pattern of belief. Eric's father, while devastated at his son's impending death, always took time to chastise him.

As his son lay dying, he said, "I told you—if you were gay, you would go straight to hell."

At one point, I looked at the father and said, "Well, Eric has fulfilled your belief for you. I wonder: if you had told him that God would love him no matter what, would he have chosen Satan to be his master?"

When his time for transition came, I was there. As he crossed, his soul left his body with palpable fear. I see whatever the person I'm helping perceives, and Eric experienced Satan as described in the Bible.

Enveloped in darkness, as though I had been dipped in black ink, I could taste the fear in my mouth—pure fear. I was thankful for the depth of faith that I had in my own beliefs. Everything resides in either a God state, which is pure love, or a fear state. The opposite of love came for Eric, and it was challenging for me as a spiritual being. Yet it was his choice, and I was glad, at the end, to be able to respect that.

≈

I received a request to work with a seven-year-old girl, Alexandria, in western Michigan, who was dying from cystic fibrosis. Her mother was a drug addict, her father an alcoholic. Before I left, I could feel myself receiving directions from Father, and took my Bible when I went to see her.

Alexandria was fascinated with the brocade that surrounded my Bible. She'd never been to church, and had never heard of Jesus. She knew about Winnie the Pooh, though, and she loved the little bear. So I told her a little about Jesus, and then we sang Kenny Loggins's "House at Pooh Corner."

We alternated talking about Jesus and singing "House at Pooh Corner," right up until her time came to cross over.

As she lay in my arms, gasping her last breaths, I glanced around the room. Her mother slouched in a drug-induced trance, not seeming to notice her daughter's impending death. Her father had passed out in the living room hours before. While I waited with her, comforted her and removed her fear, Jesus appeared and told her he was waiting for her, and took her in his arms.

I could have told her about Buddha or Abraham or anyone else, or shared with her that Winnie the Pooh would come for her, and it would have happened exactly that way. I'd picked Jesus because that was my comfort zone, but it wasn't necessary to stick to any one deity. Since she was so young, and her family didn't participate in this part of her passing, it was left up to me. Had the family expressed a preference, then we'd have spoken about that.

I left the brocade so that it could be buried with her body.

23

WHAT IS GOD?

GOD IS NOT A being sitting on golden throne, saying, "Well, only twelve people prayed for you, and fifteen people prayed for someone else, so I'm going to let you die." Nor is God waiting with fire and brimstone, ready to dole out punishment. God and the Other Side, like all things, carry only the meaning that we give them. It is what it is. Period.

God is nothing *and* He is everything.

Mankind has a tendency to separate this world, including the afterworld, into us and them. There is no separation, however. When we die, we are exactly the same. We are in different energy forms when we lose our cellular structures, our bodies, but we remain right here.

Some people say they talk to the dead, and relay messages from dead people to their grieving relatives. They read the vibrational signature of the person who has transitioned, and do an awful lot of creative interpretation. They say what they think the person might be saying.

They might say, "It's your cousin Bob, and he's very angry," or, "Your mother is happy." Yet human emotion does not exist on the Other Side. A soul cannot experience human emotion outside the human body experience. The Other Side is the absence of emotion. We try to assign feelings and emotions to it, so that *we* can understand it, but the Other Side is pure logic.

The Other Side is a state of complete serenity. No anger, resentment, or jealousy resides there, nor does any joy, laughter, or pleasure. These are human emotions that have no bearing on the Other Side. How can a soul be angry, or happy? That is pure judgment.

The Other Side is here, but most of us don't see the vibrations of souls who have transitioned. We use religion, the paranormal, and the phenomena as ways to make ourselves feel special. Serenity exists on the Other Side . . . a thousand times more profound than anything you'll ever experience in human form.

Throughout my lifetime, during times of severe personal unrest, I've always taken a pillow and blanket and gone into the deepest, darkest closet in my home . . . not because I'm depressed, but because in absolute blackness, I can see my own light inside of me, and truly understand that God is within me.

The Creator is not some untouchable, unreachable object. He is a part of you, in you, existing inside of *you*!

I worked with a man in his mid-thirties named David. He had appendicitis, and his appendix had burst before it could be removed. It was also cancerous, and the cancer had spread throughout his abdomen.

David and his wife, Marie, were both executives, and had been married ten years. They'd put off having babies in order to travel the world extensively. Marie had become pregnant just months before David developed appendicitis.

His belly grew even as his wife's belly grew with their baby, for as the cancer spread throughout his abdomen, it grew more and more swollen. In time, it split open.

Marie was frantic for a cure, and they went to Mexico and Germany for help. The baby was born, and David kept getting worse. That's when he contacted me.

We did a Cellular Cleansing, and when we reached his age eight, it was clear that his soul had a contract, that it was to be released from the human form at age thirty-eight.

David decided to rewrite his contract, and I watched as he changed the age of his death to seventy-four. However, when I asked him to verbally read his contract back to me, he said the age of his transition would be thirty-eight.

At that point, I knew his soul was going to go. As gently as I could, I posed the question, "Why are you still around?"

"For Marie and the baby. She'll be so devastated if I die."

We discussed the pros and cons of being true to himself, and being true to his wife. We rationally looked at the trauma that she, and the rest of their families, would endure if he indeed spoke to them of how he truly felt.

Ultimately, after much discussion, he made a decision: he would tell her that he wanted to go.

We told her together. It devastated her, and she cried hysterically. I could only imagine the pain that conversation had caused as she left the room.

Marie returned a few hours later, having been able to accept David's decision. She had been the one searching for and researching cures. She had made all the trip plans. She had initiated all the desperate measures they'd attempted.

Now, she truly understood that he was not participating in his own healing. He was going through the motions to pacify her.

One night near the end, Marie called and asked me to come be with David the next day. He got on the phone with me and was clearly delusional. When Marie got back on the phone, I said I would come down first thing.

The next morning, as I ate breakfast with my sons, Father quietly spoke to me. "You told my son David that you would be with him when he crossed. He is now ready to come home."

I was a hundred miles away, so I said to my boys, "I have to leave my body for a little while. I'll be back in fifteen minutes or so. Everything is okay. I just need to help this man transition."

While I don't speak a lot of my sons in this book, I'd like to note that they have been incredible young men. While living with me was indeed different than what their friends experienced, they never judged me, or questioned the length of time I was gone from them throughout the years, as I assisted other people. My leaving my body to go assist a soul crossing was just another normal day for them.

I left my body and went to David, and helped his soul leave his body and transition to the Other Side. David and Marie had just become Christians, and had little understanding of the belief, but they had a wonderful Minister who'd helped prepare them for this challenging transition.

As I arrived in soul form, I could see David's grandparents had come for him, as had Jesus. I helped David by connecting my vibrational essence to his soul, and assisted him with the final release of the physical form, and then I returned to my body, back in my house in Hartwell.

As soon as I popped back into my body, my telephone rang. Marie said, "It's David. We're trying to do CPR. Please do something!" The anguish in her voice was devastating.

"I already did," I said quietly. "It was time for him to go home."

I immediately got in my car and drove the 100 miles to their home, and spent the day with Marie. She wouldn't eat unless I helped her, and wouldn't sleep unless I held her hand. I stayed with her throughout the day, and we talked about her need to refocus. After all, she now had a beautiful six-month-old baby boy to raise.

For years, I received Christmas cards from Marie as her beautiful son grew. She and David will always hold a special place in my heart as an incredibly courageous couple.

Another morning in Virginia Beach, as I ate breakfast with my then-boyfriend Tony, a soul reached out for me, requesting assistance. When this happens, and it often does, I have to make a decision. Should I sit at the table and help the soul find its way naturally, simply by offering the soul access to my vibration, or should I excuse myself from whatever it is I'm doing, and call my office to find out who has called for help, and work directly with that person or their family?

In this case, the soul would make its connection without my full attention, so I began to eat my omelet.

"What just happened?" asked my boyfriend.

"What?"

"You stopped in mid-sentence, and didn't say anything or respond for half a minute. Your eyes went blank, and it was clear you didn't comprehend anything I said."

I explained to him what had happened, and asked if it bothered him.

After a few minutes of thought, he said, "Hmmm, I think I'll just equate it to your pager going off!"

He was the first man in my life to call this "lapse" to my attention. People have since brought it up, but he was the first one to notice it and say so.

While every soul has a contract dictating what it will learn and accomplish while it is in human form, it is unusual to have a contract such as David's, agreed to at age eight. Usually, we have three or four checkout points in our life. These are various times when the soul would be permitted to transition, once it has learned the lessons it was contracted to learn, and accomplished what it was put on the earth in its human form to do.

If a soul has not yet done what it was intended to do, it cannot give up its human form. In a near-death experience, the soul comes out of the body and re-enters through the soul tunnel, and reconnects with the Divine Spark. There is a moment of checks and balances. If the soul has completed its tasks and learning, it can stay reunited with the Divine Spark. If it has not, it disconnects from Source, shoots through the tunnel, and goes back into the body through the heart center.

A few years ago, I went to Oregon to help Katherine, a twenty-six-year-old woman with cystic fibrosis, transition to the Other Side. She didn't fear death, but she was terrified of drowning in her own body fluid—her lungs were almost paralyzed with thick mucus. I promised her I would come to her as her time got closer, and remove the fluid from her lungs so she could die of congestive heart failure.

I removed the mucus from her lungs, and began feeling it entering into my own body. She quit gurgling with every breath, and breathed easily and quietly. Then she peacefully died from congestive heart failure, as I'd said she would.

Her parents became brutally enraged with me. "If you could help her breathe, then why didn't you save her life?"

"God didn't tell me to save her," I said. "I can't save someone unless He tells me to."

People have unrealistic expectations of individuals with true gifts. I'm simply a conduit, with the ability to get my own thoughts out of the way so that Father can do the work that needs to be done on a physical level. I don't have the will or the capability to make those types of decisions. The Universe is in charge, not me. I can only do what I am told to do. Joao in Brazil can't make decisions as to who lives or dies.

If someone tells you they have that capability, you need to just walk away, because they are not people of integrity. None of us has that capability, that power. Only the Universe, Father, Mother, God, Creator, All That Is, All That Will Be, has that knowledge.

Katherine's parents are still furious with me to this day, but I could not interfere with her soul's contract with God. Most people, being too close to the departed, don't look at it that way—again, unrealistic expectations.

An equally important lesson for me was learning not to take such recriminations personally. Of course, as a mother, I might feel differently if I didn't know what I know.

People have faith and belief in their lives when things are going well, but when they perceive that things are going poorly, that faith and belief goes out the window. They want control, and to micro-manage the situation.

My work with someone is not about whether they live or die, it's about whether their soul had a growth experience because of their interaction with me. Did a soul grow and learn? If so, then dying, or transitioning, is not a negative outcome.

A 57-year-old nun called me. She'd been diagnosed with stage-three breast cancer. In between hysterical crying, she said, "I still have so much I want to do. There's so much work for me to do."

As she continued to cry, I posed this question: "Which part of your illness am I supposed to feel sad about?"

She abruptly stopped crying. "I beg your pardon?"

"You're in a win-win situation," I said. "You're a woman of strong faith. If you have a remission from cancer, then you get to stay in this human form a bit longer. If you don't, you get to go home. Again, which part of this should I feel sorry for?"

After a moment of dead silence, she started laughing and said, "I never thought of it that way."

Many times my work is not about curing disease, but about my patients arriving at an understanding, about their coming to peace with what is taking place. The nun above had followed what she felt God had asked for her entire life, and now that he was possibly asking her to come home, she was going to fight him, argue with him, and disobey him?

24

THE DIVINE SPARK

WE ALL CAME FROM the same place at the exact same time. We are all spiritual peers, like babies who have just been born. All of us, as souls, splintered from the Divine Spark at the same moment.

How did we become this dense flesh?

When we first came to this planet, we were high vibrational beings, like angels and spirit guides are now. We developed a thought process. Thought is everything. Then we began developing emotions. Our original state of Unconditional Love is that state of the Divine Spark. We then shifted into the lower vibrations of anger, jealousy, resentment and fear. Finally, we developed a form—skin, bones, and organs—so that we could live on this planet in this state.

We are vibration and geometry. That's it.

When I look at you, I see your true form, which includes everything you've ever experienced. When I walk into a room, I see everyone who has ever been there, and all of their experiences. As my sight has changed, it's harder to see people in the form of a human being.

When someone speaks to me, I start to make out their vibrational form separate from the rest of what is going on in a room. As I look at someone, I see everything that has happened to them in the same second. I always ask them to tell me what is going on right now, personally, physically and professionally. As they speak, the vibrational patterns and blockages that most need attention show themselves to me, in various forms: images, movies, smells, sensations, and actual words.

When someone makes you angry, that emotion goes directly into your body, not the body of the person making you angry. The truth is, no one can make you feel anger or resentment. *You* choose to experience your reaction, and your choice determines what goes into your body, vibrationally. When an emotion plugs the subtle energy field, it slows down your vibration.

Most people in the world believe, and most religions generally propagate, that when human beings die, they leave their bodies behind and reconnect with Source. They leave a place of judgment and ego and move into a state of Unconditional Love. However, we do not have to die to reach this unconditional state. We can do so while still in human form. All we need to do is raise our vibrational level by removing blockages/words from the subtle energy system, and keep it moving free and clear.

We can live in a balance between our right and left brains, our intuitive and intellectual sides.

Do not underestimate the vibrational power of the spoken word. As people speak, words go directly into the actual cellular structure of the body. It is fascinating. I could sit and watch people all day, observing what they say going right into their bodies. The word is another way in which we create a blockage in the subtle energy field. Thoughts go into the auric field, words go into the subtle energy field, and the written word goes into both. The body does not know discernment. It makes literal truth out of everything we say.

So what are we waiting for? How do we move out of judgment? How do we become insubstantial without transitioning? From this moment forward, we watch our emotions, our words, our thoughts, and we work diligently to remove stored emotions/words already within our body by utilizing an active vibration.

Human beings have two energy systems. The auric field is outside the body and includes the Chakra system. Most alternative energy medicine practices deal exclusively with auric fields. Healing modalities that work on the human energy field, such as Reiki, crystals, and Therapeutic Touch, involve the auric field only.

Inside the body flows a separate energy called the subtle energy system. This is the form in which we first existed, when we first came from the Divine Spark. It's more commonly known as the immune system, only it doesn't exist the way we think it does.

Why do we need an immune system? Many people reply, "To protect the health of our bodies." But would Source give us something to fight with, given that life is perfect? Would it be necessary, from an all-loving being?

No.

The immune system is actually the subtle energy field. Unlike chakras, which were created to accommodate our slowing vibrational forms, the subtle energy system has been a part of us since the very beginning.

When we are born, we are fully sighted and aware of the other words going on around us that most adults do not see. We perceive Angels and Spirit Guides all around us. We trust in our ability to know without question, because at birth, the thymus gland is fully functioning. Located in the center of the chest, in the Heart Center, it's our physical connection with Source and with our subtle energy system.

In Biblical times, it was not uncommon for people to live hundreds of years. The Yogis lived that long, because their subtle energy vibration was much faster than ours is today. They experienced few blockages in the subtle energy system, and enjoyed long spans of good health as a result.

Ancient humans used to live in their right brains, guided by intuition. As we evolved, as our vibration slowed down and our forms became denser, we learned not to trust ourselves. We began to rely on our left-brains to tell us how to live, and how to act, utilizing the right brain only occasionally. As we created emotional blockages in our vibrational forms, disease spread and we died younger.

These vibrational blockages are passed on, from the subtle energy systems of one generation to the next, in the DNA of the cell.

Five components comprise the key to understanding our connection to the Divine Spark within each of us.

The Heart Chakra

All chakras are not created equal. The Heart Chakra, or Heart Center, is in the auric field. Our souls did not come to this physical form with a Heart Chakra or any of the others; they developed as our vibrations slowed.

The Heart Center is located in the center of the chest. Many people can sense the energy there with sight or temperature. Some modalities, such as Reiki, work to balance and clear the Heart Center, and while such methods can offer temporary relief of systems, they don't remove the cause of the imbalance or blockage.

When we experience anger or fear, our Heart Center shuts down and becomes smaller. When we close off our Heart Center, we literally close off our connection with Source, or the Divine Spark.

The Thymus Gland

The Heart Center is directly connected to the thymus gland, and the thymus is our physical connection to Source, or the Divine Spark within each of us. When we are born, our thymus gland is large and fully functional. The size of an infant's fist at birth, it usually atrophies after puberty.

We are born fully sighted and fully intuitive to the worlds unseen by most adults. Angels and Spirit Guides are seen in their true form and not differentiated from souls in human form. Have you ever noticed a toddler, cooing and smiling, pointing at the ceiling, seemingly at nothing?

As we grow up and are taught by adults not to trust our inner knowing, our thymus gland shrinks and becomes dormant. Current thinking suggests the thymus becomes smaller because we do not need it physiologically as adults. Actually, it atrophies from lack of use. When we stop trusting ourselves and our intuition, the thymus shuts down. As we learn to stay out of judgment and reconnect with Source, the thymus activates again.

The thymus gland, which sits behind the sternum in the center of the chest, is our physical connection to the Divine Spark within. In fact, the name thymus derives from the Greek *thymus*, which refers to that which pertains to the soul.

The thymus, hypothalamus, and spleen comprise the organs of the immune system, or subtle energy system.

In our bodies, the hypothalamus acts as a kind of computer inside the body. Found behind the pineal gland and behind the nose in the brain, its job is regulating our subtle energy system, and determining how much the heart center can handle. Like a computer, the hypothalamus must have data for it to perform its function. With no data entry, the hypothalamus cannot function well.

The spleen is connected to the thymus. As you raise your vibration and activate the thymus, energy is abundant. The spleen stores that energy.

I've known some healers to leave their bodies in order to work with clients. They leave through the back of the head or the crown chakra. When I work with a patient, I occasionally bi-locate, and a carbon copy of myself leaves my body, but not through the crown chakra—it leaves through the spleen.

I've spent many hours talking with ancient individuals about the spleen connection, trying to understand it. There's a star tetrahedron in the spleen, and when enough high vibrational energy has been stored in the spleen, a carbon copy of me leaves my body through the star tetrahedron. Even people who cannot feel energy around people's bodies have told me they feel the cone of energy that comes out of my side when I duplicate myself. If I bi-locate to a wall, and people touch the wall, I can feel them as if they are touching my actual body.

It is much less painful to bi-locate at will, rather than if I am called to help someone and it just happens.

When the thymus, hypothalamus, and spleen are all fully connected and activated, it becomes absolutely clear that serenity is everything. There is nothing beyond serenity when the subtle energy system is flowing and unobstructed with low vibration.

The Subtle Energy Field

The subtle energy field is the energy system that goes through every single cell in your body. In science, we call this the immune system.

Every word you've ever spoken travels along this high-way system throughout your body. If you're speaking in true Unconditional Love, then your words strengthen this system. If you are in conditional love, then your words travel into the cells and "stick." They eventually condense and become disease, and your immune system suffers, and your body continues to deteriorate.

Many times, you're totally unaware that there's a problem within your body.

The Soul

Beyond the subtle energy system is the soul, or the higher self. The soul is our individual personality of spirit, created the moment it split from Source.

One day, a woman in a workshop said to me, "I am fully connected to my higher self."

"That's good," I said.

She then said she was going through a divorce, was on drugs, and had an alcohol problem. She wanted to know how she could be connected to her higher self and still have what she perceived to be problems.

The soul is more divine than you will ever be, consciously. However, one of the biggest pieces of misinformation out there is that the soul is your perfect self, and that if you are fully connected to your soul, you'll have calm serenity in your life, and everything will happen the way you want it to happen.

This is not true.

The soul is imperfect. If your soul were in a state of serenity, fully connected to Source, then why would you be here? The soul exists in human form to learn, not to provide answers. The higher self does not automatically have all the solutions. In order for the soul to learn, the universe must get our attention, most often in ways that manifest as illness or relationship issues.

The soul can learn in two ways. One is sitting on the side-lines, existing outside of human form, and watching people interact. It slowly absorbs what it needs to know through observation.

The second method is coming to this earth in human form and living a life. Our souls learn much faster as active participants than as observers.

Since our souls are here to learn, no matter what happens, you cannot make a mistake. Everything is simply a learning experience, nothing more and nothing less.

When the soul splits from Source, it makes a contract at that instant. The contract determines what we are to learn, and how we are to serve while in human form. Each of has our own contract with Source. None of us knows the contract of another soul, and that, quite simply, is why we must not judge another person.

Most of us do not know what our own soul's contract is with Source. We do not know what our mission or purpose is on this planet.

People often come up to me and say, "Can you tell me if I am on path?"

My response is usually this: "How can you be off path? If you do not know what your path is, how can you possibly be off?"

Your soul will learn what it has been put on this earth to learn, and it will serve its purpose. You will not die until you have grown as a soul, and accomplished whatever it is you were meant to do.

What about free will?

You choose how you live. You determine how easy or difficult, miserable or joyful, your journey will be as you learn and serve.

The Dark Tunnel

Beyond the soul is a dark tunnel full of the things we dislike about ourselves. It's a part of us.

Have you ever said something really horrible to someone, and then thought, "How could I have said such a thing? That's horrible!" You were coming from your dark tunnel.

Many of us would rather the dark tunnel didn't exist. Most of us have a strong urge to get in there and clean it up, make everything "good." Another misconception. Why?

Duality must exist. We don't know how *good* we can be until we know how *bad* we can be. If we don't like this part of ourselves, if we try to change it, clean it, or deny it is even there, we stand in judgment. When we enlist judgment against ourselves, we dramatically slow our vibrational form.

We must be brave enough to go inside and look carefully into this tunnel. We must believe that we can handle anything that it shows us. Once we look at the darkest part of ourselves, we must love it unconditionally, just as we love the parts of ourselves we find agreeable and pleasant.

The one thing—the only thing—the universe demands of us is that we have Unconditional Love, and that includes for the dark tunnel.

25

UNDERSTANDING THE DIVINE SPARK

WHEN OUR AWARENESS passes through the dark tunnel, we see the Divine Spark. It's the piece of Source inside every one of us. In the Divine Spark, judgment does not exist, nor does ego. The only sensations are Unconditional Being and a sense of absolute serenity.

Most people walk around about thirty-five percent connected to Source. I'm usually about seventy percent connected. I don't trust myself to connect more at this point; I don't trust myself to come back.

When I talk in front of a group of people, I slow my vibration down to match theirs. This process requires a great deal of effort and is quite tiring. However, if I don't do it, people are exhausted, feel flattened to their chair, or overcome with emotion. That's why work with a patient over the phone is easier for me—I don't have to shut that connection down so much. I can let my energy and connection with Source remain at seventy percent without overwhelming the person on the other end of the line.

163

In my work, I've sat with and observed many clients while they died and transitioned. At the moment of death, the soul comes out of the body momentarily. Then it shoots right back in—through the heart center, through the tunnel, into the Divine Spark they've always carried in their bodies. At that time, they're reunited completely with Source, reaching a state of non-judgment and non-ego, and they experience complete unconditionalism.

People who've had near-death experiences often describe a sensation of coming out of their bodies, then going through a dark tunnel toward a bright light of total peace and serenity. In a near-death experience, the soul goes through the tunnel and reunites with the Divine Spark, just as in death. However, since the person is meant to live, the Divine Spark and the soul separate and return to their respective places.

Increasing Your Awareness

It's simple to increase your intuitive abilities, once you understand the role of the thymus and the other energy components of the heart center—and you understand the Divine Spark. As with most new skills, it just takes a little practice. First read through these instructions, and then try it for yourself.

1. Close your eyes. On your forehead, above and between your eyes, is your third eye, the purpose of which is intellectual intuition. Concentrate on your third eye.

2. Imagine a gold chain dropping down from your forehead into your heart center, in the middle of your chest. Slowly lower your third eye down the chain into the heart center.

3. Imagine your heart chakra becoming bigger and your heart center more open.

4. Sit quietly and use the intuition of your third eye as it perceives your environment and your body. When you remove the intellectual component of the intuition, you can become aware of your perceptions without any judgment or ego.

〜

A good intuitive utilizes one or two senses. A great intuitive uses all five. Be open to your body giving you messages through your heart center—through sight, touch, smell, taste and hearing. Be aware of any symbols or images it may use to communicate.

One woman at a workshop became fully sighted while doing this exercise with a partner. In her excitement, she called me over and said, "I can see a book in her rib cage!"

"That's good," I said. Interestingly, the woman's book was written right to left.

I continued to work with other students in the class. Fifteen minutes later, I returned to the woman, who was still staring at the other woman's chest.

"What are you doing?" I asked.

"Reading the book," she said.

"Is it your book to read?" We all laughed.

"No, it isn't."

"Your job is to help her read her own book," I said. "When you work with clients, your role is to help them understand the messages from their bodies, not to do it for them. The message isn't for you. It's not yours to interpret. Your job is to give them the information, without your input, and let them decide what it means."

Although the woman had the best of intentions, she hadn't learned to respect the process of the other woman's soul.

We must not use our intuition to intervene on another's path, or read someone else's book.

Approach everything in your life as you perceive it in your heart center. When you look at other people, look at them through the heart center's Unconditional Love. Be open to any senses or symbols your body uses to communicate with you intuitively. Make it a practice that you do not do anything in your life unless you are absolutely coming from your heart center.

26

COLORWORKS

COLORWORKS IS A visualization process that uses active vibration within your body to release or heal specific symptoms, emotions, or physical challenges.

Begin ColorWorks by closing your eyes and taking three deep breaths. Consciously make yourself aware of your body, and relax it. Imagine wrapping a loving white cocoon of mist loosely all around you.

In the next step, you must choose a color, but not consciously. Even if you don't "see" the color, rely on your body— your subconscious mind—to choose the exact shade of color, represented by its vibrational rate, to assist with your specific request. Your body will take less than one minute to choose and give you the color you need.

When asking your body what color it needs, be specific about the task and location.

· What color do I need to remove this heavy grief from around my heart?

· What color do I need to remove this sharp pain in my lower back?

· What color do I need to release this tightness and stress from my neck and shoulders?

· What color do I need to dissolve this cyst from my right underarm?

· What color do I need to increase and improve access to my memories?

· What color do I need to allow myself to accept forgiveness for _____?

· What color do I need to increase my feelings of self-worth?

· What color do I need to release my long history of "failure" and accept success?

· What color do I need to release my automatic thought response of judgment?

· What color do I need to increase my confidence by 80%?

· What color do I need to increase my energy by 75%?

The more specific you are in your description of intensity, and location in your body, the more specifically your body responds. Whether you wish to remove a negative feeling from your entire body, or heal an infection in your right ear, remember to *be specific*. There is no wrong way to do this. Listen to your internal guidance.

1. You may have many different ways to move the color through your body. For example, on the inhale, pull the color through the bottom of your feet, then move the color through your body, picking up the negative energy, and blow the color and what it has collected out of your mouth. Or imagine releasing it through the crown Chakra while you're blowing out through your mouth, whichever is easier for you. Inhale briskly, and exhale like you're blowing out a candle. Concentrate on the fact that bits of the negative issue are leaving with the color each time you exhale through your mouth.

2. While releasing negative issues from your body, accept that the color, will change quite a bit, and at times you may have two or three colors entering at the same time. Continue moving colors until the color goes back to white on its own. If after you still have many different colors after ten minutes, then *you* take the color back to white yourself, by visualizing the mist as all white.

3. Draw the white in through your feet, using all your pores, until it fully engulfs you in a healing, cleansing white light filled with Unconditional Love. While moving the white light through your body, express your appreciation aloud, as though you were in perfect physical and emotional health already:

   a) "Body, I love you unconditionally."
   b) "Body, I accept you fully as you are."
   c) "Body, I thank you for being clear and healthy."
   d) "Body, I am accepting . . . love, forgiveness, healing . . . ."

Say an affirmation appropriate for your situation.

4. Ask your body, "What color do I need to fully balance?" This may be any combination of colors, from a rainbow to only white. Breathe in through the bottom of your feet as you inhale, bringing this color through your body, and release by shooting the color through the top of your head—your crown Chakra. Do this exercise for one minute, then quietly walk for a minute or two to let your body adjust to the new vibration.

5, You may choose to journal any emotions or thoughts after the session. ColorWorks "homework" usually requires exercises twice a day for ten days, then once a day for the next twenty days.

Using the process of ColorWorks® will continue to benefit your health and well being. Give yourself fifteen precious minutes every day, and it can change your life.

Questions and Answers about ColorWorks

My clients have asked me many questions about the ColorWorks process. Following are the ones that come up most often.

"I don't visualize, so right from the beginning I had a problem doing ColorWorks. I couldn't visualize myself wrapped in a cocoon of white light, or visualize the colors moving through my body. How can I do the exercise if I cannot visualize?"

Many people visualize well, so the exercise is given in that form. If visualization is not something that comes easily for you, then one of the following examples will align with your dominant sense to assist you in accomplishing the same purpose, with a variation of ColorWorks.

Remember these following sensory paragraphs are only an outline to suggest a framework for you, so you can customize the process to the thoughts or descriptions which will have meaning, and which will bring the most effective results *for you.*

1. *Visualize* – Not creative within your visualizations? Don't worry, for they often flourish with practice. You can borrow and customize advertisements, or memories of things you've actually seen, to enhance your visualization abilities. In the beginning, when the white cocoon is forming, the mist arrives just as easily as mist produced for a stage production, but it feels like being wrapped safely in your comforter or duvet. A number of automobile advertisements show a car in a wind tunnel, with faint mist flowing around and past it, to demonstrate its aerodynamic design. You can imagine your body as the car, and the mist, moving slower, flowing not only around you, but through you as well. Each time you inhale, the mist becomes thicker and more vibrant in color. It moves easily inside you, picking up the particles that will release through your mouth when you exhale. When it's time to balance, the colors that move up through your body and release out the top of your head move quickly—just like a little fireworks display!

2. *Kinesthetic* – If you are more kinesthetically inclined, then you will feel the colors. Feel yourself wrapped in the safety of white, within its glowing strength and power. Then imagine an actual "feeling association" between the color your body has chosen, and the positive effect it provides you. Feel a warm and gentle release as the color moves through and out your mouth. Deeply feel yourself responding to the color as it

lifts and carries away particles. Feel lighter as the color frees you from your issue, or feel fuller and satisfied as the color gives you the relaxation and comfort you've asked for. Feel each moist, warm exhale softening and releasing your issue, as the active colors move through your body.

3. *Hear* – If your most dominant sense is hearing, then hear the different colors. Hear the white as it enfolds you in its pure, protective, loving tone. White might carry the deep, rich tone of a heavy bell for you, which, once rung, carries the note clearly as it harmonizes your body. The warm [use your own adjective here] tone of the color your body needs to assist you deepens its tone, as it collects particles and moves through your body. Imagine that your exhale clears each tone brought through your body. Imagine your body vibrating in perfect harmony with the white of balancing, just as though your body was in sync with a tuning fork of perfect pitch, when your body's balancing is completed.

4. *Smell* – Imagine the white surrounding you as having the same fresh, comfortable smell of being wrapped in your favorite clean duvet or sweater. Imagine the smell of the new color as though it were mist in the air, or microscopic particles of baking soda. Let it move from the bottom of your feet and up through your body, absorbing any negative smells as you release blockages, and exhale them through your mouth. The final balancing will bring a smell that represents harmony and balance to you.

5. *Taste* – Imagine the white surrounding you as containing the sharp, clear crispness of a fresh apple, or perhaps the

sweetness of marshmallow sauce. As the tiny white micro-scopic particles move through you, the taste of them changes and enhances you. Your body's color of release may have the subtle taste of a citrus sorbet, which becomes faint as it collects and releases your negative issues. The final balancing to harmony could be represented by a color hinting of a delicate balance, like a gourmet sauce simmered to perfection.

6. *Know* – When guided by a sense of knowing, definitive thoughts come easily to you. Know that you're relaxed and safe, wrapped in white. Know that the colors are moving through your body as you guide them. Know the exhale of your breath is clearing and healing your body physically and emotionally. Know deep in your cells that the rebalancing stage allows your body to fully incorporate the vibrational changes you've made.

7. *Direct Internally* – If none of these options sound like they fit with your style, then you can always mentally talk yourself through the process. Simply say each step to yourself inside your mind. For example, "I am now surrounded by a cocoon of white light." Once you've determined what color you need, continue by saying, "Purple is moving up through my feet, and continuing up my legs and abdomen. The purple is now in my chest. The purple has changed shades of color as it has collected bits of negativity and is bringing them along. The purple is carrying the negativity out my mouth." Concentrate on taking deep breaths on both the inhale and exhale, as you move the color.

"When I did the exercise, an area of the body came to mind, and a color seemed to be suggested, but I wasn't certain that was really happening. I felt as though I could have been making it up. How do I know these were correct?"

Who knows more about you than you? One of the reasons I want to share this wonderful ColorWorks system with you is to help you realize that you're totally empowered. You have the abilities within yourself to move forward, into a healthy, balanced, happy and productive life.

All the answers, all the information you need about what is best for you, is within you. You need just two things: a way to access the information inside you, and the belief that you're capable of doing it. As you use this technique the realization that you're capable will develop.

Illness and disease are simply a result of storing painful memories. Once you learn how to recognize the cause of pain, and remove it, you'll be able to improve your health. Illness, disease and imbalance need not exist within you.

"I did the exercise, but nothing happened!"

It may seem as though nothing is happening, but that's not the case. Something changed. You may not be able to perceive at this time what changed, or where it occurred, but something did shift.

Continue doing the ColorWorks process. In about a week, you'll be aware of the change. It would also be helpful for you to write down your thoughts and feelings right after doing the work. Take ten minutes, and write down whatever comes to your mind at that moment.

Don't judge what you write, and don't try to correct or edit it. The writing is for you alone; no one is going to grade it. At the end of the week, read what you've written. You'll be surprised at the pattern that emerges. It will lead you to an insight about yourself.

"I couldn't breathe the way you described, and at the same time move the colors the way I'm supposed to. What do I do?"

Coordinating all these things can be difficult, especially if it's unlike anything you've done before. Keep in mind that there's no wrong way to do the ColorWorks. If it's too hard to breathe and move the colors, then think of a way that would accomplish the same result, but be easier for you.

How about setting up a color pump? Once you know the color you need, mentally set up a pump filled with that color. Tell the pump that it's timed with your breathing. Then, as you breathe, it will pump just the right amount of color. Just focus on your breathing, and let the pump do the rest.

If that's too mechanical for your preference, then why not create a color wrap? Mentally create a wrap of the color you need, and place it on the area of the body you're working on. Then focus on your breathing. The color is in place, and will do its work.

It may require a little creativity, but you will be able to think of a solution that fits your style, and that will enable you to do ColorWorks.

"I want to work on eliminating depression. My whole body feels depressed. How do I work on my whole body?"

Depression is a good example of a "whole body" condition. Pay close attention specifically to *how you asked the question* of your body, before tuning in to your body's response.

If you ask your body where the depression is, your body will indicate that it's all through your body. However, if you ask your body where the depression is stored in your body, your body will identify a specific spot. The area your body indicates then becomes the focus of your work.

"What about other diseases that affect large areas or most of my body? What if I have a serious auto-immune condition like lupus, or arthritis, or cancer?"

You need to ask your body where your issue—disease, trauma, etc.—is stored, so you can release it from your physical body. Be aware that your body may not indicate the same area where you currently feel physical pain!

Locating and releasing the originating emotional issue from your body often removes even chronic pain, which may have been present for many years. Ask your body *when* your disease began to be stored in your body. The originating key to release a disease, such as Lupus, will usually be identified as an event with a domineering parent. Finding this event gives you a specific point of forgiveness or healing to work with.

When a parent is domineering over a child, the child often responds by pulling back, and by not fully being himself. As a result, the child chokes off the free flow of energy within his body. Then, since the body doesn't get the energetic nourishment it needs, it creates a disease that appears to be everywhere.

"Why do I have to turn the cocoon back to white? Why can't I just leave the cocoon the color my body said it needed?"

White is most effective in cleansing and clearing out the body, even though the color your body requests breaks up the blockage and gets it moving. If you have any experience doing laundry, think of white as the fabric softener in a rinse cycle. White perfectly finishes the work done within you, after the color your body chooses to use as "detergent" is complete.

"Why must I do the affirmations even if I'm not 'well' yet?"

The whole purpose of the ColorWorks, after releasing your issue, is to establish within you new and positive thought and word patterns, so you do not re-create your issue. Colors release blockages, but the affirmations are insurance against continuing to use the same thought and speech patterns that created your issue in the first place. When you regularly think and speak in new and positive ways, it helps you make a habit of your new pattern of appreciation, and more quickly.

"When I asked my body what color it needed to get rid of my headache, I thought it said black! Does that mean I have a brain tumor?"

No, your body isn't saying you have a brain tumor. Black is not a bad color; it doesn't mean something bad is taking place. Color is simply a convenient way of recognizing and using vibrations, and no one color is better than any other.

Your body simply needs the vibration of black. Black is a heavier and slower moving vibration, which is effective at breaking large or solid blockages into manageable pieces.

"Does one color work better than another?"

I suggest you begin the ColorWorks by wrapping yourself in a white cocoon simply because white is a color that most people feel safe with. If you feel safer in pink or yellow, then use one of those colors at that point, but remember to rely on your body's choice of color to deal with your issue, as it is not the visual shade of color that's important, but its vibrational quality must match what your body needs to work.

"The second time I did The ColorWorks, I asked for a color, and the answer I got was triangles. Did I do something wrong?"

You cannot do ColorWorks "wrong." Triangles are just fine. Your body knows what it needs. Shapes have their own vibrations.

One client, a little boy about six, told me he needed purple triangles with lime green centers. He started breathing them through his body, and all went well for about a minute. Then he started to sneeze. When I asked him what was going on, he said the triangles tickled!

"Why do I have to ask for a color to balance my body?"

The old saying, "Nature abhors a vacuum," applies here. You have moved out chunks of old energy, and that work has left tiny, empty spaces, and a new vibrational rate. You need to replace what you've released, and stabilize it with something new and preferable; otherwise, the old pattern will return.

The balancing color, along with the affirmations, move in to set the new pattern in place.

"I felt cold when I did the ColorWorks. Is that normal?"

I get cold, too. When you move that much energy, directing your body's resources to that specific task, they're no longer focused on keeping you warm. Keep a blanket handy, and wrap up before beginning, if you need to.

"After I did the ColorWorks, the room was really stuffy. Why was that?"

What you're recognizing is the old, stale energy you've just moved out. To help remove it from your environment, I suggest using curry. Put about an inch of water in a small sauce pan, bring it to a boil, and add one tablespoon of curry. Stir it gently for a few seconds, and then walk around the room where you've been working. Direct the steam into the corners of the room.

While you're at it, why not give yourself a fresh beginning by walking throughout the entire house, cleaning out stale energy from the corners of each room with your curry pot?

"Is there anything I can do to help deal with a difficult situation in the moment, so it doesn't get stored, instead of needing to do the full ColorWorks process later?"

You're looking for first aid, and that's a great idea. If you're in a challenging situation, use your time and energy to make what improvement you can in the moment by touching or massaging your comfort spot. Later you can handle the balance when you do the ColorWorks process completely.

Everyone has a Comfort Spot, which, upon being touched or rubbed, helps you feel more comfortable. Some people have two. If you don't know where yours is, have a friend stand about five feet away from you and, beginning at the top of your head, visually scan your body. He should very slowly scan your forehead, across your eyebrows, your eyes, and the bridge of your nose, and so on, right down to your toes. As he does this, he will hit on one spot that makes you smile. That's your Comfort Spot.

If nothing shows up on the front of your body, it may be necessary to turn around and have your friend scan your back side as well. Nothing says that the Comfort Spot is located on the front of your body, nor does it have to be in the easiest-to-reach location.

When you've located your Comfort Spot, you can use it to help clear away or prevent the internalization of negative emotions, thoughts, or issues.

For example, let's say you've just had an argument with your child about picking up his toys. He refuses to do what you ask, throws a toy at you, and runs out the back door. You're sitting in the kitchen awash in a tide of feelings—tired, frustrated, feeling like a failure as a parent, and angry that you seem to be the only one to discipline your son.

Take a deep breath, exhale, and begin to rub your Comfort Spot as you think of the scene that just took place between you and your son. Breathe calmly as you review it. In many cases, you'll feel a shift, and your feelings become less intense. Instead of feeling as if you've just run into a wall, you may find a door—a way to handle this issue—or you may have the feeling that you'll find a solution soon. Later, when you have time to do the full ColorWorks process, you can do a more thorough job of clearing the anger and the feeling of failure.

The Comfort Spot can also be used as a tool to help you clear old memories and emotions. The process is much the same as for handling the previous issue. Think of an issue in the past that still causes you stress. Once you have the issue clearly in your mind, and you're feeling the emotions that go with it, rub your Comfort Spot, and continue until you feel a shift.

The feelings may lighten a little, they may lighten a lot, or the whole issue may leave. You can think of it and feel neutral, as if you don't have an emotional attachment to it. This is an especially good way to deal with stressful issues. Rubbing the Comfort Spot helps loosen them up so that, when you're ready to do the ColorWorks process, these stressful memories will move out more easily and completely.

"What if I want to clear out a stressful issue, and it's evident that my body isn't ready to let go of it. What do I do then?"

When you can be in a calm place, think of the issue. Ask yourself why you're not ready to let go of this particular issue. As an answer comes to your mind, press gently on your heart, and ask if that's the real reason you're not ready to let go. When you come to the true reason you're still holding onto the issue, you'll feel a shift inside yourself. You can then decide the best way to deal with it.

"I do not 'see' the actual colors my body chooses on the inside of my eyelids, or I only see colors every now and then. Am I doing ColorWorks wrong?"

ColorWorks cannot be done "wrong." If you do not ever "see" the colors, you may simply be processing through another dominant sense. If you see colors only occasionally, your dominant sense may change from time to time, or even from day to day. The most important part is to trust the process.

27

CELLULAR CLEANSING

WHILE COLORWORKS EFFECTIVELY releases blockages from, and re-balances, your cells for as long as you continue to use the process, it works at a steady and cumulative rate.

In the 1990s, I began working on a technique capable of rapidly releasing a larger percentage of the blockages held in cellular memory, within a much shorter time frame. I developed and refined the Conklin Method of Cellular Cleansing. Cellular Cleansing is capable of allowing you large releases—40-60%— of the blockages held within your cellular memory, all within an intense day-and-a-half process, and often with dramatic healing results!

Following this paragraph is the information I ask my Certified Associates to present, when assisting their clients in determining whether Cellular Cleansing would be appropriate for them.

Cellular Cleansing Can Improve Your Health

Even if you had a happy childhood, your subconscious mind is almost certainly limiting your physical and emotional health right now. Don't worry, because there *is* something you can do about it!

Appreciate the perfection you already are.

Your body is an amazing healing machine. When you were born, you knew how to heal yourself. No one taught you, yet you could heal a cut or mend a broken bone. Stitches or a cast do not cause healing to begin; your healing response is part of your cellular memory. Reproduction of perfect cells is in your cellular memory.

Why Do We Need Cellular Cleansing?

Throughout your lifetime, your body has kept a perfect copy of your every word, thought and emotion. They're stored in your cellular memory. As a result, you've become what you say, think and feel. Over time, many layers of emotional memories have developed into blockages, interrupting your body's flow of subtle energy, weakening your immune system.

Your body's cells are always in one of two modes: grow or protect. To continue good health, cells need to reproduce in grow mode. When in fight or flight response, adrenaline and chemical surges switch your cells into protect mode. When you say, "Aunt Zelda has cancer, and she may die," you've unconsciously created an emotional roadblock for yourself.

Your subconscious mind cannot distinguish between your hopes and fears, the past and present, or internal and external sources. Everything you say, or think, is real, It's happening now, and it's all about you. Your body absorbs the words "cancer" and "die," and processes their emotional impact in protect mode, as though *you* are in danger. Your body has processed in this manner since your childhood!

Why Me?

You and I have virus and cancer cells in our bodies, and we have genetic predispositions. What activates these and other diseases? It's simple: your beliefs govern your health.

Your ability to set and maintain healthy perceptions is the key to your physical and emotional wellness. How you see, feel, and digest—literally absorb into your cells—is based upon your perception of life, and your perception is within your control to change.

Your mind and body are not separate. Your beliefs, and every emotional word you've spoken regarding anyone's life, have *all* been absorbed inside *you* . . . into your cellular memory. This increases your vulnerability to diseases becoming active, and slows your natural recovery response once a disease process has begun.

Make Better Choices

1. Be aware of your beliefs and of your power to choose words.

2. Change your perception. Focus on the positive aspects of any situation. Ask yourself what you've learned.

3. Remove thought patterns that aren't to your emotional benefit, including the unknown fears and outdated self-protection programs currently running in your subconscious mind, through Cellular Cleansing.

What are the Benefits of Cellular Cleansing?

The wonderful thing about this process is that you don't deal with old memories. You don't have to remember *anything*, because your body has all the knowledge to access every memory. You keep the memories of your life, but you release the painful emotions, allowing healthy growth to occur.

The majority of clients experience a notable shift in physical wellness after choosing the Conklin Method of Cellular Cleansing. Clients have found this to be a wonderful way to let go of their past issues, improving their lives today. You, too, can gain a whole new way of looking at life after Cellular Cleansing!

Cellular Cleansing has provided truly amazing results for many people, but it's not a magic bandage. Even when you make an unmistakable shift in your physical and emotional health, you *must* do your homework in order to keep the wonderful changes you've achieved!

Your homework is a series of specific visualizations appropriate for your situation, similar to those used in Color-Works, but involving the use of the Pools found at the close of the Cellular Cleansing process.

Returning daily to the Pools, for a set period of time, consciously reinforces your choice to incorporate into your body *only* your new and positive ways of thinking of, feeling about, speaking about, and looking at, your life. You can choose to change your way of perceiving your body, your relationships, and your surroundings, every day.

Questions and Answers about Cellular Cleansing

"What is Cellular Cleansing like?"

The process of Cellular Cleansing is a detailed, specific, guided visualization that begins by having you relax. I ask you to visualize a flight of beautiful white marble stairs. As you reach the bottom, you see a glorious hallway filled with doors. Each door represents one year of your life. As you mentally open the door to each room, you see that the room is dirty— no people or memories, just dirt. Then you see your Angel or Guide, and together you clean the room. As you clean, you're literally cleaning out the blocked energies and stored memories within your body.

I lead you to each room and provide directions. You keep memories of your life, but you release the painful emotions such as fear, anger, resentment, orjealousy, enabling you to look at your life in a whole new way.

The day before a Cellular Cleansing, I usually connect energetically to you, and send a vibration of chaos to begin loosening the blockage within you. This allows the maximum release in the actual Cellular Cleansing process.

The first afternoon of a Cellular Cleansing usually goes no further than clearing the room up to age six or seven, yet releases the largest amount of blockages.

Most of our beliefs and issues, including the way we've chosen to perceive ourselves and the world around us, are stored within these years. Although the time used to release issues from your body is only a few hours on the first day, it's normal to feel drained by the large shift in your vibrational rate, so I ask you to not plan any type of active program for yourself. An Epsom salts bath and sleep is always good.

I continue to stay connected energetically to you over this evening, pulling energetically on your issues or disease, and processing what you release.

The second day of Cellular Cleansing covers the larger linear time frame of your life. The rooms are then organized to clump your life into small groups of three to five years.

The close of Cellular Cleansing is a series of Pools, which are powerful and give you specific tools and choices. Your body responds by dealing not only with your past, but with your physical and emotional wellbeing today . . . and in your future, as well.

You have the power within yourself to change your perceptions, and you were born with the knowledge to heal yourself. ColorWorks and Cellular Cleansing both clear blockages and disease from your physical and emotional vibratory rate.

"Is Cellular Cleansing for me?"

Ask your body if this is appropriate for you. If you receive a tightening or a sinking feeling, then take it as a "no" at this time, and set is aside. If your body responds with a light feeling or a flutter, then take it as a "yes," and schedule an appointment.

It's always important to listen to your body. It has all the answers. Trust it completely, because only *you* know what is right for you.

APPENDIX

Patti's Version of Vibrational Medicine
by Melanie Boock, R.N.

[A dear friend, Melanie Boock, R.N., assisted me with this appendix. She has the unique advantage of working with western medicine as a registered nurse in an emergency room, while at the same time learning extensive alternative methods such as therapeutic touch, Reiki, Cellular Cleansing, ColorWorks, etc.]

WHEN SOMEONE COMES TO my emergency room in the middle of the night, doctors often start their investigation with the cell. The C.B.C., or complete blood cell count, is one of the most frequently ordered tests.

Blood contains several cells: red (erythrocytes), white (leukocytes), and platelets (thrombocytes). In a C.B.C., the cells are counted, and the distribution of the various types are evaluated. The count of white blood cells is further detailed into the number of cells that are in various states of maturity. White blood cells are especially important, as they conduct the primary work of the immune system. When an infection is detected by the body, it increases production and release of leukocytes. Some white blood cells are also phagocytes, which means they remove a virus or bacteria from the body by literally wrapping themselves around it, engulfing it, and consuming it.

When a patient undergoes surgery to remove an unusual growth, that tissue is carefully contained and sent to a pathology lab for further examination of its cells. The doctors there ask a few key questions, a few of which are:

1. Is this normal?

2. Is this abnormal but harmless?

3. Is it malignant or benign?

For those with conventional vision, the ability to see cells under a microscope is absolutely essential to appropriate diagnosis. It's impossible to imagine practicing modern medicine without the ability to see individual cells, as well as cells as a group.

The importance of the cell in diagnosing illness has long been respected and relied upon in medicine. In recent years, actual altering of the cell, other than by removal, has gained more acceptance and popularity in therapeutic modalities. The emergence of stem cell research has proven especially promising, as in 1998 a technique to grow and duplicate stem cells was developed. The idea that stem cells can be physically recreated an infinite number of times, and each time, a different type of cell can be created from it, is incredibly promising to the medical community.

Another vital component of medical science is the diagnostic applications of physical energy. Several examples that provide invaluable information are Radiographs (X-rays), Computed Tomography (CT) scans, Magnetic Resonance

Imagining (MRI) scans, and Ultrasounds. The machines utilize various energetic frequencies, and are interpreted by computers, displaying an image based on the information obtained by measuring energy absorbed, reflected, or produced by the body.

In addition to diagnostic applications, machine-made energy is commonly used in therapeutic practice. A defibrillator delivers a brief shock of electricity to a heart that is quivering uncontrollably. Radiation therapy delivers a specifically-aimed beam of energy to shrink a tumor. TENS (Trans-Cutaneous Electrical Nerve Stimulator) units send electrical impulses through electrodes placed on the skin in order to interrupt nerve pathways and give relief to those who experience chronic pain.

While Patti Conklin's methods may seem confusing, they simply utilize the same building blocks, cells, and energy that western medicine depends on every day. As Patti says, "Everything is vibration and geometry. Everything."

In both medical practice and Conklin's practice, cells are the geometry, and various forms of energy comprise a vibration. When Conklin's Cellular Cleansing is used, it works on the individual's actual cells. The client is induced into a light hypnotic state, and they are asked to visualize entering a room that represents a certain age. The practitioner then suggests cleaning the room and envisioning it as the client would like it to be.

The room is a metaphor for a cell, and items or clutter the individual sees in his imagination are actually memories inside the cells of his or her body.

Patti's vision allows her to see that the emotional memory as a peptide, or a protein chain, inside of the cell. It does not belong there, and therefore is causing a disruption. The memories' energy is an actual, physical peptide, and thus the link between the mind and body. In these instances, the slow vibration of the emotion has become a physical form.

Patti and her trained practitioners simply raise the vibration of the peptide so it can leave the cell. As it passes through the cell membrane and into the person's body, Patti takes it into her own body, just as a white blood cell engulfs any foreign protein, such as a bacteria or virus. In addition, with a Conklin Method Cellular Cleansing practitioner, you yourself may experience flu-like symptoms for a few days as your cells release emotions and words.

Patti notes that most of her clients feel tired, sore, and may have a mild fever after a Cellular Cleansing. This is because our own bodies mount an immune response, as it has also recognized the peptide as foreign. She insists they take Epsom salt baths to sooth this response, and rest for several days.

Patti's particular application of vibrational medicine is unique. However, numerous forms of vibrational healing have been utilized ever since we began to vibrate at a slower frequency, and exist in a physical body.

There are two types of healing through vibration: passive and active.

Passive vibration affects the auric field, which is an energy field that exists outside of, and around, the body. Thoughts go into the auric field, and spoken words go to the subtle energy field, or immune system, as discussed briefly in Chapter 2. Written words go to both.

Many forms of passive vibration are utilized by practitioners and clients alike, to great success in balancing the auric field. They include, but are not limited to: Reiki, Therapeutic

Touch, Herbal Medicine, Bach Flower Essences, Crystals, Magnets, and Homeopathy. All have therapeutic value. None, however, can actually remove energetic blockages from the subtle energy system, just as none can remove the core emotion or memory which is causing a disruption in the auric field.

The auric field mirrors what is *taking place* inside the immune system, rather than the *actual cause* of our symptoms. In other words, it mirrors the cancer, or it mirrors the lymphoma, but not the cause of these diseases.

The common misconception is that rebalancing the auric field will remove the causative blockage. It won't, not even close. However, techniques that restore and revitalize the auric field *do* act as bandages and aspirin—they'll cover up the problem, and they'll remove some of the pain, and the passive vibration of many alternative therapies provides a wonderful range of symptom relief.

Still, they don't remove the causative agent.

"What we call the immune system is really the subtle energy system," Patti states again. Spoken words and written words go into the subtle energy field, inside the body. Only *active* vibrations, such as color or sound, can remove these energetic blockages. Only color and sound can remove the emotion, word, memory, or specific cause of a slow, out-of-sync vibration.

Dr. Bruce Lipton is a cellular biologist who has made remarkable advances in discovering where and how the mind/body link exists. He has been a quiet, reasonable voice who contradicts the popular, pseudo-scientific idea of genetic determinism.

Some scientists believe genetic determinism is the idea that every person's health, disposition, temperament, IQ, motivation, and station in life are solely and completely dependent on his genes. Lipton notes, however, that his research has repeatedly shown genes cannot turn themselves on and off. A gene must be *on* in order to express itself. Many scientists feel there is significant evidence to show that an outside influence does, indeed, activate genes, but they don't know how. Most suspect a combination of environmental factors, including chemical exposure, ambient radiation, pollution, or hormones. However, Lipton notes in his essay, "Insight into Cellular Consciousness," that vibrational forces *can* activate a gene:

> "Conventional biomedical sciences hold that environmental 'information' can only be carried by the substance of molecules (Science 1999, 284:79-109). According to this notion, receptors only recognize 'signals' that physically complement their surface features. This materialistic belief is maintained even though it has been amply demonstrated that protein receptors respond to vibrational frequencies. Through a process known as electro conformational coupling (Tsong, Trends in Biochem. Sci. 1989, 14:89-92), resonant vibrational energy fields can alter the balance of charges in a protein. In a harmonic energy field, receptors will change their conformation. Consequently, membrane receptors respond to both physical and energetic environmental information." (Lipton, Bruce. Bridges ISS-SEEM Volume 12, No. 1, 2001.)

Lipton's work supports Conklin's statement—color and sound are the only active vibrations capable of removing a vibrational blockage. In his book *The Biology of Belief*, he states: "When you want to enhance rather than stop atoms, you find vibrations that create harmonic resonance. Those vibrations can be of electromagnetic or acoustic origin." (118)

Patti emphasizes that color, in and of itself, has no emotion. It simply represents different frequencies of an electromagnetic spectrum. In many alternative energy modalities, color seen in someone's aura is said to represent different states of physical and mental health, good or bad. However, color is simply a particular wavelength. It doesn't mean anything.

Patti has often stated that she rarely sees auras, but one that she did see was of a Japanese monk. It was completely black. She described his 'beautiful energy' as fully in balance. Black, in his case, was a state of pure energetic harmony.

Patti's observations through the years have repeatedly demonstrated that cells exist in one of two modes: growth or protection. Her vision enables her to see what other scientists see, only without a microscope. Growth or protection. That's it. And Lipton describes his experiments with endothelial cells—found in the lining of blood vessels—that yielded similar results.

When the mind perceives a threat, and experiences a sensation of fear, the body responds by releasing chemicals that spurs a fight or flight reaction. Adrenaline courses through the blood, raising the heart rate and blood pressure, and causes vasoconstriction in the extremities in order to move blood toward vital organs. The mechanisms of the body's life are halted as it prepares to flee or mount an attack on the perceived threat.

Patti believes there are only two states of being: fear and love. All other emotions and experiences are derivatives of these.

Fear

When the mind experiences a form of fear, our bodies receive a message to shut down. The cells assume a defensive stance by going into protection mode. These cells become 'soft,' and more vulnerable to the forces of their environment.

Growth

Cells in a growth mode are reacting to an experience of love. This includes any type of unconditionality, or states of non-ego and non-judgment.

Like Patti, Lipton's experiments with endothelial cells showed changes in their membranes—prompted by two chemicals released in a moment of fight or flight— as they responded to their environment. According to him, cell membranes have two switches for both chemicals. One chemical, histamine, produced a localized immune response. Lipton found that the histamine receptor, located on the cell membrane, had two switches.

1. One activated a protection response when it encountered histamine, and the cell retreated.

2. The other activated a growth response, and the cell moved toward the histamine.

Lipton found that cell behavior was the same when exposed to adrenaline, the other chemical produced in a fight or flight response, as the membrane again had two receptors for the chemical. Like the histamine, it produced the same results—one receptor activated a growth response, and the other a protection.

One type of receptor responded to adrenaline, and the cell went into a protection mode and retreated. If the other receptor was activated, the cell demonstrated growth behavior. Adrenaline is produced as a whole body response, rather than a localized one, as was the case with histamine release. Lipton found that adrenaline receptors took priority over histamine receptors when influencing a cell's behavior.

In an emergency department, patients sometimes are afflicted with a life-threatening condition called anaphylactic shock. It is a severe allergic reaction, and the body is essentially shutting down in order to protect itself from a perceived threat to its integrity. It does so by releasing massive amounts of histamine. The standard of care in treating anaphylactic shock is an injection of adrenaline, also called epinephrine. People who have experience anaphylactic shock are encouraged to carry Epi-Pens with them at all times, which is a device used to make injecting adrenaline into one's own body possible while somewhat incapacitated. As Lipton showed in his endothelial experiment, cell behavior is determined by both adrenaline and histamine receptors that trigger either a growth or protection response. Adrenaline overrides histamine receptors when determining cell behavior.

Lipton demonstrated that cell behavior mimicked the behavior of entire organisms, such as the human body. Adrenaline acted like the mind of an organism, influencing cell behavior over the commands of the local histamine production, which mimic the body. The mind thus influenced the body. Lipton was ecstatic about the implications of his experiment, but his colleagues were mortified at the suggestion of cell behavior illustrating the mind-body connection in a biological context. He subsequently published his paper without heralding the most exciting discovery of his experiment, but later documented his observations in Biology and Belief thirteen years later.

Dr. Richard Gerber, M.D., is another individual whose explorations and research in vibrational medicine has caused suspicion and disrespect from his some of his peers of the western medical establishment. When Dr. Gerber, who practices internal medicine, first published his definitive text on energy-based healing called *Vibrational Medicine* in 1987, he considered doing so under a pseudonym. He did use his real name, and his book is in its third printing.

In his book, he states "Medical researchers do not yet understand that the subtle energy system flow of prana through the heart chakra is an integral factor in the proper functioning of the thymus gland and, thus, the body's immune competence."

Patti has observed the importance of the thymus gland to a healthy immune system in her own work. Infants and children have a fully functioning thymus gland in the center of their chests. It is generally accepted in medicine that as children grow into adults, they no longer need the thymus. It shrinks and disappears. Patti's vision showed her real reason the thymus shrinks and ceases to function. Children trust in their own knowing; the trust the answers that come from their bodies via the thymus gland in the heart center. As they grow and are conditioned by adults to trust others above their own knowing, such as doctors, teachers and even parents themselves, they begin to doubt themselves. They doubt what they have always known to be true. As children grow into adults and look to external clues such as the advice of other people, no matter how knowledgeable or well-intentioned, the thymus gland deteriorates from inactivity.

Patti sees the subtle energy system, or the immune system, as a hanging plant in the middle of the heart center. The plants system of branches and leaves flows throughout the entire body. As one doubts his own knowing, the plant wilts and sags. As one increases his ability and inclination to listen to the answers of his own body, the plant flourishes and appears lush and green.

The mind-body link continues to gain respect and credence in the realms of medical science. Recent studies that have quantified a correlation between the incidence of illness and the emotional state, attitudes and spiritual practices. Patti and other researchers have noted that eastern medicine emphasizes preventing disease, and western medicine is more effective in treating disease once it has occurred. As she states, duality must exist. Applications of both types of medicine are essential. Vibrational medicine is currently utilized by both types of medicine. Alternative applications include promotion of health or relief of symptoms through vibrational therapies, such as acupuncture, Therapeutic Touch, crystals, and homeopathy. Western medicine primarily utilizes vibration in diagnostic machines such as CT scans and MRI scans, and in some therapies, such as radiation therapy.

Western medicine is not short on miracles in its own right, especially in terms of treating trauma. There is no vibrational equivalent to cross-clamping an aorta to prevent someone who is bleeding to death from a car accident or a gunshot wound. As an emergency room nurse, it is quite a miracle to apply a defibrillator and deliver an electric shock that restores a normal heartbeat and restores life.

Where trauma care is the most dramatic and accelerated area of modern medicine, other areas of healthcare, such as wellness and prevention, languish behind. Patti's vision gives medicine a window into the mind-body link, and an opportunity to make great strides in improved delivery of care. As someone who makes a living, hour by long hour, in the heart of Western medicine, I am as grateful to be a part of it as I am exhausted at the end of the day. While it is probably politically incorrect to say so, the part of my job I love the most is starting an IV and injecting fast-acting opiates and anxiolytics that give patients instant relief from pain, and a feeling of well-being.

Becoming familiar with Patti's work over the years has not changed my own sight or abilities. It has made me a better nurse as I realize that every patient I see has his or her own path. As Patti says, do I know that soul's contract with God? Of course not. Then may I judge that person? The more I can stay out of judgment, the better I do my job in the realm of western medicine in an emergency setting. As anyone who works in an ER will say, we see the worst of what people can do to each other. It is a great challenge to stay out of judgment. I still have a long way to go, in terms of consistency.

Patti makes clear is that the concept that everything is vibration and geometry is not an adjunct to other practices. Conversely, it is the central principle to which everything else is an adjunct.

ABOUT THE AUTHOR

PATTI CONKLIN is described by clients and colleagues as one of the greatest medical intuitives of the 21st century. Patti was born with a rare vision and vibrational capabilities. Receiving her first visitation from God at the age of seven, she was put on a path of being of service. After high school she began international non-profit work, daily utilizing and expanding her gift throughout her life until she received yet another visitation at the age of thirty-eight and was instructed by God to fully begin walking the path that she was asked to walk as a child. Having absolute faith, five minutes later she resigned from her non-profit director position. A month later she moved to Georgia as instructed and began her work. She has been assisting and teaching people since that blessed day.

She has been mentioned in many books, some being *Miracles of the Casa* by Josie Ravenwing, a book about John of God in Brazil; *Soul Agreements* by Dick Sutphen; and *Radical Remission* by Dr. Kelly Turner to name a few. She has received numerous awards and acknowledgements through the years by many institutions, including her honorary Ph.D's in Divinity and Humanities for her life's work. Patti has a private practice and is an instructor at the International Metaphysical University. Her work with clients, allopathic and alternative physicians, and her teaching is worldwide, having reached more than forty countries.

RELATED TITLES

If you enjoyed *God Within*, you may also enjoy other Rainbow Ridge titles. Read more about them at *www.rainbowridgebooks.com*.

The Divine Mother Speaks: The Healing of the Human Heart
by Rashmi Khilnani

The Cosmic Internet: Explanations from the Other Side
by Frank DeMarco

Conversations with Jesus: An Intimate Journey
by Alexis Eldridge

Dance of the Electric Hummingbird
by Patricia Walker

Coming Full Circle: Ancient Teachings for a Modern World
by Lynn Andrews

*Afterlife Conversations with Hemingway:
A Dialogue on His Life, His Work and the Myth*
by Frank DeMarco

*Consciousness: Bridging the Gap Between Conventional Science
and the New Super Science of Quantum Mechanics*
by Eva Herr

Jesusgate: A History of Concealment Unraveled
by Ernie Bringas

Messiah's Handbook: Reminders for the Advanced Soul
by Richard Bach

Blue Sky, White Clouds
by Eliezer Sobel

Inner Vegas: Creating Miracles, Abundance, and Health
by Joe Gallenberger

When the Horses Whisper
by Rosalyn Berne

Channeling Harrison, Book 1
by David Young

Lessons in Courage
by Bonnie Glass-Coffin and don Oscar Miro-Quesada

Your Soul Remembers: Accessing Your Past Lives through Soul Writing
by Joanne DiMaggio

Rainbow Ridge Books publishes spiritual, metaphysical, and self-help titles, and is distributed by Square One Publishers in Garden City Park, New York.

To contact authors and editors, peruse our titles, and see submission guidelines, please visit our website at *www.rainbowridgebooks.com*.